Lecture Notes in Computer Science   13194

Sridutt Bhalachandra · Christopher Daley ·
Verónica Melesse Vergara (Eds.)

Accelerator Programming Using Directives

8th International Workshop, WACCPD 2021
Virtual Event, November 14, 2021
Proceedings

Springer

Editors
Sridutt Bhalachandra 🆔
Lawrence Berkeley National Laboratory
Berkeley, CA, USA

Christopher Daley 🆔
Lawrence Berkeley National Laboratory
Berkeley, CA, USA

Verónica Melesse Vergara 🆔
Oak Ridge National Laboratory
Oak Ridge, DE, USA

ISSN 0302-9743 ISSN 1611-3349 (electronic)
Lecture Notes in Computer Science
ISBN 978-3-030-97758-0 ISBN 978-3-030-97759-7 (eBook)
https://doi.org/10.1007/978-3-030-97759-7

LNCS Sublibrary: SL2 – Programming and Software Engineering

This Springer imprint is published by the registered company Springer Nature Switzerland AG
The registered company address is: Gewerbestrasse 11, 6330 Cham, Switzerland

Preface

In today's high-performance computing (HPC) environment, systems with heterogeneous node architectures providing multiple levels of parallelism are omnipresent. Architectures are evolving rapidly as we speak. Nodes in a future exascale system may also consist of GPU-like accelerators combined with other accelerators to provide improved performance for a wider variety of application kernels. The accelerators have become more usable in recent years, often providing high bandwidth memory with sufficient capacity to fit more of a scientific application's working set, hardware-managed caches, and the ability to implicitly access CPU data without the need for explicit data management. As a result, scientific software developers are being offered a rich platform to exploit the multiple levels of parallelism in their applications.

With increasing complexity to exploit the maximum available parallelism, the importance of programming approaches that can provide performance, scalability, and portability is increasing. Historically, the favored portable approaches, and sole focus of our earlier workshops, were OpenMP offloading and OpenACC. Today, we recognize there are other options and have extended the workshop to include use of standard Fortran/C++, SYCL, DPC++, Kokkos, and Raja among several others that can provide scalable as well as portable parallel solutions without compromising on performance. It is highly desirable that programmers are able to keep a single code base to help ease maintenance and avoid the need to debug multiple versions of the same code.

These proceedings contain the papers accepted for presentation at the 8th Workshop on Accelerator Programming using Directives (WACCPD 2021)—https://www.waccpd.org. WACCPD is one of the major forums for bringing together users, developers, and the software and tools community to share knowledge and experiences when programming emerging complex parallel computing systems.

As in previous years, the workshop highlighted improvements to the state of the art through the accepted papers and prompted discussion through keynotes that drew the community's attention to key areas that will facilitate the transition to accelerator-based HPC. The workshop aimed to showcase all aspects of heterogeneous systems, discussing innovative high-level language features, lessons learned while using directives to migrate scientific legacy code to parallel processors, compilation, and runtime scheduling techniques, among others.

The WACCPD 2021 workshop received 11 submissions out of which seven were accepted to be presented at the workshop and published in these proceedings. The Program Committee of the workshop comprised 24 members spanning universities, national laboratories, and industries. Each paper received a minimum of three single-blind reviews. A new role of "Proceedings/Reproducibility Chair" was added to further help with the reproducibility initiative. This role was ably filled by Ronnie Chatterjee from Lawrence Berkeley National Laboratory. Similar to WACCPD 2020, we encouraged all authors to add the Artifact Description (AD) to their submissions and make their code and data publicly available (e.g. on GitHub, Zenodo, Code Ocean) in support of the reproducibility initiative. As a further push, only papers with AD were considered for the Best Paper Award. Of the seven accepted papers, two had reproducibility information and these manuscripts are highlighted with an 'artifacts available' logo in this book.

The program co-chairs invited Barbara Chapman from Hewlett Packard Enterprise (HPE) to give a keynote address on "New Frontiers for Directives". Barbara Chapman was a Professor of Computer Science for over 20 years, performing research on parallel programming interfaces and their implementation. Currently at HPE, she is defining future directions for the HPE Cray Programming Environment but remains affiliated with the Department of Computer Science and the Institute for Advanced Computational Science at Stony Brook University, where her team is engaged in efforts to develop community standards for parallel programming, including OpenMP, OpenACC, and OpenSHMEM.

Mathew Colgrove from NVIDIA Corporation and Sunita Chandrasekarn from the University of Delaware gave an invited talk titled "Introducing SPEChpc 2021". Mathew Colgrove is an NVIDIA DevTech engineer working with the NVHPC compiler team. Mat is also NVIDIA's representative on SPEC's CPU and HPG benchmarking committees. As well as serving on SPEC's Board of Directors, Mat holds several officer positions including Release Manager for SPEC HPG and SPEC's Vice-President of Operations. Sunita Chandrasekaran is an Associate Professor with the Department of Computer and Information Sciences at the University of Delaware, USA. She is also a computational scientist with Brookhaven National Laboratory. She received her Ph.D. in 2012 on Tools and Algorithms for High-Level Algorithm Mapping to FPGAs from the School of Computer Science and Engineering, Nanyang Technological University, Singapore.

The workshop concluded with a panel on "Publicly-available directive test suites for heterogeneous architectures" moderated by Christopher Daley from Lawrence Berkeley National Laboratory. The panelists included

- Swaroop Pophale, Oak Ridge National Laboratory, USA
- Michael Kruse, Argonne National Laboratory, USA
- Brandon Cook, Lawrence Berkeley National Laboratory, USA
- Mathew Colgrove, NVIDIA Corporation, USA
- Rahulkumar Gayatri, Lawrence Berkeley National Laboratory, USA

Based on rigorous reviews and ranking scores of all papers reviewed, the following paper won the Best Paper Award. The authors of the Best Paper Award also included reproducibility results to their paper, which the WACCPD workshop organizers had indicated as a criteria to be eligible to compete for the Best Paper Award.

- Miko Stulajter, Ronald Caplan, and Jon Linker from Predictive Science Inc.: "Can Fortran's 'do concurrent' Replace Directives for Accelerated Computing?".

An honorable mention for Best Artifact Description/Artifact Evaluation was presented to

- Kohei Fujita, Yuma Kikuchi, Tsuyoshi Ichimura, Muneo Hori, Lalith Maddegedara, and Naonori Ueda from the University of Tokyo, Riken, and the Japan Agency for

Marine-Earth Science and Technology: "GPU porting of scalable implicit solver with Green's function-based neural networks by OpenACC".

These winners received prizes sponsored by NVIDIA Corporation.

Like last year, 2021 was (unfortunately) again a challenging year, as the world is trying to recover from the devastating effects of the COVID-19 pandemic. Major events around the world were canceled or scaled-down. Most computer conferences switched to virtual or hybrid formats. To this end, Supercomputing 2021 was held in a hybrid format for the first time. Similar to last year, WACCPD 2021 was again a fully virtual workshop. Thanks to all of you that contributed to its success! Hopefully, we will be able to meet in person again next time. Stay tuned!

December 2021

Sridutt Bhalachandra
Christopher Daley
Verónica Melesse Vergara

Organization

Steering Committee

Rosa Badia — Barcelona Supercomputing Center, Spain
Barbara Chapman — Stony Brook University, USA
Oscar Hernandez — NVIDIA Corporation, USA
Kuan-Ching Li — Providence University, Taiwan
Nick Malaya — AMD, USA
Duncan Poole — OpenACC, USA
Jeffrey Vetter — Oak Ridge National Laboratory, USA
Michael Wong — Codeplay Software, UK

General Chairs

Sunita Chandrasekaran — University of Delaware, USA
Guido Juckeland — Helmholtz-Zentrum Dresden-Rossendorf, Germany

Program Chairs

Sridutt Bhalachandra — Lawrence Berkeley National Laboratory, USA
Christopher Daley — Lawrence Berkeley National Laboratory, USA
Verónica Melesse Vergara — Oak Ridge National Laboratory, USA

Proceedings/Reproducibility Chair

Ronnie Chatterjee — Lawrence Berkeley National Laboratory, USA

Publicity Chair

Rahulkumar Gayatri — Lawrence Berkeley National Laboratory, USA

Web Chair

Weile Wei — Louisiana State University, USA

Program Committee

Daniel Abdi	National Oceanic and Atmospheric Administration, USA
James Beyer	NVIDIA Corporation, USA
Maciej Cytowski	Pawsey Supercomputing Center, Australia
Johannes Doerfert	Argonne National Laboratory, USA
Rahulkumar Gayatri	Lawrence Berkeley National Laboratory, USA
Antigoni Georgiadou	Oak Ridge National Laboratory, USA
Millad Ghane	Samsung Semiconductor Inc., USA
Priyanka Ghosh	Pacific Northwest National Laboratory, USA
Arpith Jacob	Google, USA
Haoqiang Jin	NASA Ames Research Center, USA
Mozhgan Kabiri Chimeh	NVIDIA Corporation, UK
Vivek Kumar	Indraprastha Institute of Information Technology Delhi, India
John Leidel	Tactical Computing Laboratories LLC and Texas Tech University, USA
Ron Lieberman	AMD, USA
Chun-Yu Lin	National Center for High-Performance Computing, Taiwan
Meifeng Lin	Brookhaven National Laboratory, USA
Simon McIntosh-Smith	University of Bristol, UK
Stephen Lecler Olivier	Sandia National Laboratory, USA
Tom Papatheodore	Oak Ridge National Laboratory, USA
Thomas Schwinge	Mentor Graphics, Germany
Gregory Stoner	Intel, USA
Volker Weinberg	Leibniz Supercomputing Centre, Germany
Rengan Xu	Dell, USA
Charlene Yang	NVIDIA Corporation, USA

Contents

Directive Alternatives

Can Fortran's 'do concurrent' Replace Directives for Accelerated Computing?

Miko M. Stulajter$^{(\boxtimes)}$ ⓘD, Ronald M. Caplan ⓘD,
and Jon A. Linker ⓘD

Predictive Science Inc.,
9990 Mesa Rim Road Suite 170,
San Diego, CA 92121, USA
{miko,caplanr,linkerj}@predsci.com
http://www.predsci.com

Abstract. Recently, there has been growing interest in using standard language constructs (e.g. C++'s Parallel Algorithms and Fortran's do concurrent) for accelerated computing as an alternative to directive-based APIs (e.g. OpenMP and OpenACC). These constructs have the potential to be more portable, and some compilers already (or have plans to) support such standards. Here, we look at the current capabilities, portability, and performance of replacing directives with Fortran's do concurrent using a mini-app that currently implements OpenACC for GPU-acceleration and OpenMP for multi-core CPU parallelism. We replace as many directives as possible with do concurrent, testing various configurations and compiler options within three major compilers: GNU's gfortran, NVIDIA's nvfortran, and Intel's ifort. We find that with the right compiler versions and flags, many directives can be replaced without loss of performance or portability, and, in the case of nvfortran, they can all be replaced. We discuss limitations that may apply to more complicated codes and future language additions that may mitigate them. The software and Singularity/Apptainer containers are publicly provided to allow the results to be reproduced.

Keywords: accelerated computing · OpenMP · OpenACC · do concurrent · standard language parallelism

1 Introduction

OpenMP[1] [11] and OpenACC[2] [5] are popular directive-based APIs for parallelizing code to run on multi-core CPUs and GPUs. For accelerated computing,

---

[1] www.openmp.org.
[2] www.openacc.org.

Supported by NSF awards AGS 202815 and ICER 1854790, and NASA grant 80NSSC20K1582. This work used the Extreme Science and Engineering Discovery Environment (XSEDE) Bridges2 at the Pittsburgh Supercomputer Center through allocation TG-MCA03S014. It also used the DGX A100 system at the Computational Science Research Center at San Diego State University provided by NSF award OAC 2019194.

ⓒ Springer Nature Switzerland AG 2022
S. Bhalachandra et al. (Eds.): WACCPD 2021, LNCS 13194, pp. 3–21, 2022.
https://doi.org/10.1007/978-3-030-97759-7_1

they provide a higher-level approach to accelerating codes without requiring writing specialized low-level, often vendor-specific, API code (e.g. CUDA, ROCm, OpenCL, etc.). Since they mostly consist of specialized comments/pragmas, they exhibit backward compatibility, allowing a non-supported compiler to simply ignore them and still compile the code as before. This makes directive-based approaches very desirable for legacy codes, and helps to allow compartmentalized development. However, they also can suffer from incomplete vendor, hardware, and/or compiler support, make codes somewhat harder to read, and, due to their rapid development, are less future-proof than standard languages, possibly requiring occasional re-writes.

Due to the widespread adoption of multi-core CPUs and accelerators, standard languages have begun to add built-in features that may help/enable compilers to parallelize code. This includes C++17's Standard Parallel Algorithms and Fortran's do concurrent (DC) (see Refs. [6,10] for examples using the NVIDIA HPC SDK[3]). Standard parallel language features have the potential to remove the need for directives, making multi-threaded and accelerated codes fully portable across compiler vendors and hardware. However, this requires compiler support, and few have been quick to implement these features for GPU acceleration.

Here, we focus on Fortran's DC construct. The NVIDIA HPC SDK is the only compiler at the time of this writing with accelerator support using DC, while Intel has indicated plans to add such support in an upcoming release of their ifort compiler included in the OneAPI HPC Toolkit [13]. Other compilers that support directive-based accelerator offloading in Fortran include GCC's gfortran[4], LLVM flang[5], AOCC's extended flang[6], IBM's XL[7], and HPE's Cray Fortran[8], but we could not find any announced plans for these to support DC for accelerated computing in the near future[9].

In this paper, we investigate the current capabilities, portability, and performance of replacing directives with DC in a Fortran mini-app that currently implements directives for GPU-acceleration and multi-core CPU parallelism. We replace as many directives as possible with DC, testing various run-time configurations and compilers. Our mini-app currently uses OpenACC with either nvfortran or gfortran for GPU-acceleration on NVIDIA GPUs, and uses OpenMP with nvfortran. gfortran, or ifort for multi-core CPU parallelism (as well as OpenACC multi-core with nvfortran). A key portability concern is if replacing directives with DC for GPU-acceleration will result in a loss of multi-core CPU parallelism. Therefore, we test if each compiler can parallelize

---

[3] https://developer.nvidia.com/hpc-sdk.

[4] https://gcc.gnu.org/.

[5] https://flang.llvm.org.

[6] https://developer.amd.com/amd-aocc.

[7] https://www.ibm.com/products/xl-fortran-linux-compiler-power.

[8] https://support.hpe.com/hpesc/public/docDisplay?docId=a00115296en_us& page=index.html.

[9] Note that as this paper was going to press, HPE has indicated plans to support DC on GPUs.

the DC loops for multi-core CPUs. We note that for codes using non-hybrid MPI for CPU parallelism and MPI+OpenMP/ACC for GPU acceleration, this is not as much of a concern.

The paper is organized as follows: In Sect. 2, we describe our Fortran mini-app with its current directive-based parallelelization, along with the test case we use, showing baseline performance results. In Sect. 3, we describe the implementation of DC into the mini-app, first introducing its capabilities and support, and then showing examples of replacing OpenMP/ACC directives with DC, including a discussion of current limitations. Then the resulting mini-app source code versions and compiler flag options used for the tests are described. Performance and compatibility results are reported in Sect. 4 for both multi-core CPU and GPU runs. Finally, discussion on the current status of DC and its potential to replace directives is given in Sect. 5. Instructions on how to access and use our provided Singularity/Apptainer containers and codes to reproduce the results in the paper are given in the Appendix.

2   Code and Test Description

To investigate the current capabilities, portability, and performance of replacing directives with DC, we use a Fortran mini-app called diffuse that currently implements directives for GPU-acceleration and multi-core CPU parallelism. Here we describe the code, the test case we use, the computational test environment, and baseline performance results.

2.1   Code Description

NASA and NSF have recently supported a program called "Next Generation Software for Data-driven Models of Space Weather with Quantified Uncertainties", whose main objective is to improve predictions of solar wind and coronal mass ejections to investigate how they might impact Earth. This will be done by developing a new data-driven time-dependent model of the Sun's upper atmosphere. One key component of this model is the use of a data-assimilation flux transport model to generate an ensemble of magnetic field maps of the solar surface to use as boundary conditions. To accomplish this, we have been developing an Open-source Flux Transport (OFT) software suite, whose key computational core is the High-Performance Flux Transport code (HipFT). HipFT currently implements OpenACC for GPU-acceleration and OpenMP for multi-core CPU parallelism, and we are interested in replacing the directives with DC.

In order to test the use of DC, we use a mini-app called diffuse that implements the most computationally expensive algorithm (surface diffusion) of the flux transport in HipFT. diffuse's source code for the diffusion algorithm is identical to that of HipFT. The diffusion algorithm integrates a spherical surface heat equation on a logically rectangular non-uniform grid. The operator is discretized with a second-order central finite-difference scheme in space, while the time integration uses the second-order Legendre polynomial extended stability Runge-Kutta scheme (RKL2) [3,8].

2.2   Test Description

Although `diffuse` is used here as a mini-app representation of HipFT, it is also used in production to slightly smooth solar surface magnetic fields to prepare them for use in models of the corona [2]. As such, we select a real-world example of using `diffuse`, that of smoothing the 'Native res PSI map' described in Ref. [4]. This large map has a resolution of 3974×2013 in (θ, ϕ) and takes 40,260 total iterations of applying the diffusion operator to smooth. A detail from the map before and after running `diffuse` is shown in Fig. 1.

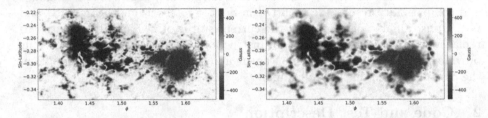

Fig. 1. Zoomed-in detail of the test case magnetic field map before (left) and after (right) smoothing with `diffuse`.

2.3   Computational Environment

In order to best assess the capabilities of the compiler support for DC, we use the latest available versions of the compilers at the time of testing. These are shown in Table 1. The CPU tests are run on the Bridges2 system located at the Pittsburgh Supercomputing Center using our allocation obtained through NSF's XSEDE program [12]. The GPU tests are run on an NVIDIA DGX A100 server at San Diego State University. Since `diffuse` does not have multi-node or multi-GPU capabilities, the CPU tests are run on a single CPU node, while the GPU tests are run on a single GPU within the DGX system. The hardware specifications are shown in Table 2.

Table 1. Compiler versions used in tests.

Compiler Suite	Compiler	Version
GNU Compiler Collection	`gfortran`	11.2
NVIDIA HPC SDK	`nvfortran`	21.7
Intel OneAPI HPC Toolkit	`ifort` (classic)	21.3

Since systems do not always have the latest compilers available, and setting up our code's dependencies can be difficult, we utilize Singularity/Apptainer containers [7]. These containers are built with the compiler environment and our dependent libraries pre-installed so they can be easily used to build and

Table 2. Hardware utilized for all test runs.

	CPU	GPU
CPU/GPU Model	(2x) AMD EPYC 7742 (128 cores)	NVIDIA A100 SXM4
Peak Memory Bandwidth	381.4 GB/s	1555 GB/s
Clock Frequency (base/boost)	2.3/3.4 GHz	1.1/1.4 GHz
RAM	256 GB	40 GB
Peak DP FLOPs	7.0 TFLOPs	9.8 TFLOPs

run the code. We use Singularity 3.8.0, and for GPU runs, use the '--nv' flag to connect to the NVIDIA driver (and CUDA library) on the local system. The CUDA run-time library used for GPU runs was version 11.4. As shown in the Appendix, running the codes in the containers yields virtually the same performance as a bare metal installation. All the test runs performed in this paper can be reproduced using the containers along with the code, both of which are publicly released in Ref. [9] and at www.predsci.com/papers/dc.

2.4   Baseline Performance Results

Our goal in this paper is to test replacing directives with DC for accelerated computing, ensuring we do not lose multi-core CPU parallelism, and that the performance is comparable to the original directive-based code. It is not our focus to compare performance between the various compilers and hardware. We therefore use similar basic compiler optimization flags (shown in Sect. 3.2) for each compiler-hardware combination and do not explore all possible optimizations. In order to compare the performance of the original code to the modified versions, we perform baseline timings of the original code. For these, and all timing results in the paper, we run each test 10 times and take the average of the full wall clock times (which include all I/O and GPU-CPU data transfer time). In Fig. 2 we show the baseline timings along with their standard deviations. We also include CPU runs on a single CPU core (serial) to illustrate the multi-core CPU parallelism. We see that each compiler obtains comparable performance on the CPU runs, yielding a speedup of $\sim 7\times$ when using 128 CPU cores compared to running in serial. While this may seem low, it is common for highly memory-bound algorithms to exhibit such non-ideal single node multi-threaded scaling [1]. The performance of the nvfortran CPU run using OpenMP is $\sim 10\%$ faster than using OpenACC for multi-core parallelism. On the GPU, the nvfortran OpenACC GPU run is $\sim 30\%$ faster than the gfortran run, which is not unexpected considering nvfortran has a more mature implementation of OpenACC.

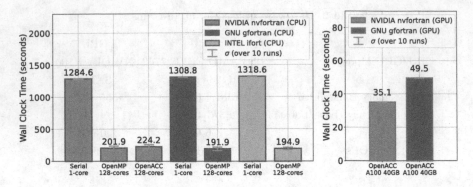

Fig. 2. Baseline CPU and GPU timing results of the original `diffuse` code run on the test case. Times shown are averages over 10 runs, and the standard deviations are shown.

3   Implementation

In this section, we first give a background on Fortran's `do concurrent` construct, and then describe our implementation of it into the `diffuse` code, and the resulting code variations. We also describe the compiler flags used for each code version and compiler combination.

3.1   The Fortran `do concurrent` construct

In 2008, ISO Standard Fortran introduced the DC construct for loops as an alternative to the standard `do` loop (or nested `do` loops). DC indicates to the compiler that the loop's iterations can be computed in any order. This potentially allows for the expression of parallelism of loops directly in the Fortran language, making it easier for compilers to parallelize the loops. While any-order execution is a necessary condition for parallelization, it is not always sufficient (for example, reduction and atomic operations, as well as others[10]). Therefore, DC can be viewed as providing a hint to the compiler that the loop is likely able to be parallelized. Work in helping make DC fully sufficient for parallelism is on-going, with Fortran 2018 adding locality statements (allowing specification of private and shared variables[11]), and specifying reductions in DC will be included in the upcoming Fortran 202X release[12].

The syntax of non-nested `do` loops and `do concurrent` loops are similar. A `do` loop has the syntax `do index=start,end` while a `do concurrent` loop has the syntax `do concurrent (index=start:end)`. The only key difference is the addition of the word `concurrent` and a small change to the loop parameters where there is the addition of parentheses and a replacement of the comma with

---

[10] https://releases.llvm.org/12.0.0/tools/flang/docs/DoConcurrent.html.
[11] https://j3-fortran.org/doc/year/18/18-007r1.pdf.
[12] https://j3-fortran.org/doc/year/21/21-007.pdf.

ellipses. With nested loops, there is more of a difference in formatting. Code 1 shows nested do loops parallelized with directives. The loop nest is shown with both OpenMP and OpenACC directives in the manner they are used in the mini-app. This nested do loop example spans 8 lines with directives, but can be written in 3 lines with DC as shown in Code 2. With DC loops, nested loops initialization statements are collapsed into one initialization statement. The syntax of DC loops is as follows: do concurrent (index1=start1:end1, index2=start2:end2, ...). As this example shows, DC loops make nested do loops more compact and easier to read.

Code 1. Nested do loops with OpenMP/ACC directives

```
!$omp parallel do collapse(2) default(shared)
!$acc parallel loop collapse(2) default(present)
      do  i=1,N
         do  j=1,M
            Computation
         enddo
      enddo
!$acc end parallel loop
!$omp end parallel do
```

Code 2. Nested do loops as a do concurrent loop

```
      do concurrent  (i=1:N, j=1:M)
         Computation
      enddo
```

Most current compilers support the Fortran 2008 standard, which includes the basic DC syntax. However, since the specification does not require that the compiler try to parallelize the loops, they are often treated as serial do loops. When a compiler does support parallelization of DC, special compiler flags are needed to activate the feature (see Sect. 3.3 for details).

Although the latest version of the OpenACC (3.1)[13] specification adds support for decorating DC loops with directives, at present, there are no implementations of this support (with the possible exception of using the kernels directive). There is also no mention of supporting directives on a DC construct within the most recent OpenMP (5.1)[14] specification. Therefore, replacing do loops with DC may break the ability to parallelize the loops when using compilers that do not support direct DC parallelization.

The current state of DC support is varied across different compilers and versions. nvfortran 18.1 added serial support for DC along with locality of variables, while nvfortran 20.11 added support for parallelization of DC loops

---

[13] https://www.openacc.org/blog/announcing-openacc-31.

[14] https://www.openmp.org/spec-html/5.1/openmp.html.

for both CPUs and GPUs. In `gfortran` 8, serial support for DC was introduced, while `gfortran` 9 added support for parallelization of DC on multi-core CPUs using `gfortran`'s auto parallelization feature. `ifort` started supporting serial DC loops in version 12. Then, in version 16, parallelization support was added through `ifort`'s auto parallelization feature (using the flag `-parallel`). With version 19.1, locality of variable support was added, and parallelization became linked to the OpenMP compiler flags. Table 3 gives a summary of the current support of parallel DC loops for the compilers used in this paper.

Table 3. Current support of DC loop parallelization for the compilers used in this paper.

Compiler	Version	do concurrent parallelization support
`gfortran`	≥9	Parallelizable on CPU with `-ftree-parallelize-loops=<N>` flag. Locality of variables is *not* supported.
`nvfortran`	≥20.11	Parallelizable on CPU and GPU with the `-stdpar` flag. Locality of variables is supported.
`ifort`	≥19.1	Parallelizable on CPU with the `-fopenmp` flag. Locality of variables is supported

3.2 Code Versions

Here we list the code variants that we use to test the portability and performance of replacing directives with DC in `diffuse`. For versions that use DC, only basic DC loop syntax was used with no locality of variables, as not all compilers support this feature in all configurations.

Original: This is the original version of `diffuse` which uses OpenACC and OpenMP directives on all parallelizable do loops as well as OpenACC data movement directives. It does not contain any DC loops. It is the code version used for the performance results of Sect. 2.4, and will be the standard we compare to for both performance and compatibility.

New: This version is obtained by replacing directive surrounded do loops in *Original* with DC loops, with the exception of reduction loops. The directives on the reduction loops are kept since reductions are not supported in parallelized DC loops (see discussion in *Experimental*). We also keep all OpenACC data directives for explicit GPU data management. This code is expected to perform as well as the *Original* code if the DC loops are recognized and implemented efficiently.

Serial: This version contains no OpenACC or OpenMP directives at all, nor any DC loops. It is the same as *Original* with all directives removed. It should run in serial in all cases, unless an auto-parallelizing feature of a compiler is utilized.

We include this code as a control and to ensure the multi-core CPU parallel runs are exhibiting the expected parallelism.

Experimental: This version does not contain any OpenMP or OpenACC directives at all, replacing all loops (including reduction loops) with DC. A key feature of this code version is that it represents the 'ideal' scenario of using only the Fortran standard language for accelerated computing without needing any directives. This version does not technically violate the Fortran standard since a DC on a reduction loop is valid if not parallelized, as the iterations can be computed in any order. However, if the compiler does parallelize these DC reduction loops, it will likely produce wrong results due to race conditions, unless it supports implicit analysis and implementation of DC reductions. As mentioned above, Fortran 202X will add reductions to DC, resolving this problem. Removing all directives also removes explicit GPU-CPU data movement, whose absence will lead to very poor performance on accelerators (due to repeated data movement between the CPU and GPU) unless the compiler supports automatic GPU-CPU memory management. Features such as NVIDIA's Unified Memory and AMD's Smart Access Memory can allow compilers to resolve this issue.

In Table 4 we summarize all versions of the code we use for our tests.

Table 4. Summary of DC and directive implementations for each version of the `diffuse` code tested.

	do concurrent	Directives
Original	None	all loops & data management
New	all loops except reductions	reduction loops & data management
Serial	None	None
Experimental	all loops	None

3.3   Compiler Flag Options

The `gfortran`, `nvfortran`, and `ifort` compilers each have different flags to implement code parallelization and optimizations. Here we describe the compiler flags we use for each code version, compiler, and target hardware configuration. For all compilers, we use the `-O3` flag to activate typical compiler optimizations, and `-march=<ARCH>` to tell the compiler to target the specific CPU we run the tests on. Typically, we use `native` for `<ARCH>` to automatically target the current system, but some configurations (such as using `ifort` on AMD EPYC CPUs) required us to specify the option manually (in that case `<ARCH>` is set to `core-avx2`). All *Serial* code versions use only these default compiler flags.

nvfortran: For GPU parallelization, the *Original* code uses the flag `-acc=gpu` which enables the OpenACC directives. We also include the flag `-gpu=ccXY, cudaX.Y` to specify the specific GPU run time and hardware capabilities (similar to `-march` for CPUs). The `ccXY` indicates a device with compute capabilities of `X.Y`, while `cudaX.Y` tells the compiler to use the `X.Y` version of the CUDA library. To check if/how the compiler parallelized the loops, we set -Minfo=accel, which outputs parallelization information.

For the *New* code (containing DC loops), we add two new flags. The first is -stdpar=gpu, which enables DC loops to be parallelized and offloaded to the GPU[15]. The other is -Minfo=stdpar which outputs the compiler's parallelization messages (similar to -Minfo=accel). When using -stdpar=gpu, unified managed memory is automatically enabled, making all allocatable arrays unified arrays. This means the runtime is responsible for correct and efficient CPU-GPU data transfers during the run, and any OpenACC data movement directives on such arrays are essentially no-ops. Static arrays are not made into unified arrays, so manual GPU data movement is still needed for good performance (note that diffuse does not make use of any static arrays). If one wants to continue to manage the GPU data manually (using OpenACC or OpenMP data movement directives), the option -gpu=nomanaged can be used.

For the *Experimental* code, since there are no directives, we simply use the standard parallelism option of -stdpar=gpu -gpu=ccXY,cudaX.Y, and rely on the compiler to automatically detect the reductions and implement them correctly, as well as manage the GPU memory using unified memory.

For CPU parallelization, the *Original* code has two implementations. One is to use OpenMP with the -mp flag, and the other is to use OpenACC with the -acc=multicore flag. Even though the OpenMP compilation produces slightly better performance (as was shown in Sect. 2.4), we only use the OpenACC multi-core option. This is because nvfortran currently activates OpenACC when using -stdpar, so we cannot use both -stdpar for DC and OpenMP (as would be needed in the *New* code) since OpenMP and OpenACC are not written to work together (and in the *New* code case, causes a compiler error). We note that when using OpenACC for multi-core CPU, the number of threads is controlled through the runtime variable ACC_NUM_CORES=<N>, rather than OpenMP's OMP_NUM_THREADS=<N>.

For the *Experimental* code, since there are no directives, we simply use the standard parallelism option of -stdpar=multicore, relying on the compiler to automatically detect the reductions and implement them correctly.

gfortran: For GPU parallelization, the *Original* code uses the flag -fopenacc, which enables OpenACC directives. In addition to this flag, the intended offload GPU must be specified. For NVIDIA GPUs, the flag -foffload=nvptx-none is used (targeting specific compute capabilities is not currently implemented). We also use the flag -fopenacc-dim=<DIM> to specify the parallel topology for the offload kernels. <DIM> is set to three colon-separated values that map to 'gang', 'worker' and, 'vector' sizes. Since OpenACC supports acceleration for multiple GPU vendors, the default values for the topology may not be optimal. Although this level of optimization is outside the scope of this paper, we observed that the nvfortran compiler was using a vector length of

---

[15] For nvfortran 21.7, it appears that setting the -stdpar=gpu flag implicitly sets the -acc=gpu option as well. This is an important consideration if one has OpenACC directives that should be ignored when using -stdpar.

128 when compiling most OpenACC loops, so as a simple optimization, we use
-fopenacc-dim=::128 for our tests. The *New* code is not supported on the GPU
with gfortran at this time. This is because there is no current support for DC
GPU offloading.

On the CPU, the *Original* code uses -fopenmp, which as above, activates
OpenMP directives for multi-core CPU parallelism. gfortran does not support direct parallelism on DC loops. Therefore, for the *New* code, we must
use gfortran's auto parallelization feature using the -ftree-parallelize-
loops=<N> flag, where <N> is the number of threads to run on. This auto parallelization analyzes both do and DC loops and determines if they can be parallelized
and if so, implements the parallelism. Therefore, it can be used in the case of the
New code, as well as the *Experimental* code. Since the compiler is auto-analyzing
the loops, it may detect the DC reduction loops and parallelize them correctly.

ifort: Since ifort does not currently support GPU-offloading with DC or
OpenACC, we only test it with CPU parallelism to ensure switching from directives to DC does not lose our CPU parallel capabilities when using ifort. For all
code versions, we add the flags -fp-model precise and -heap-arrays as those
are standard flags we use for runs of diffuse to ensure robustness and precision,
but they are not related to parallelization. For the *Original* code, we use the flag
-fopenmp in order to enable OpenMP directives to produce parallel code for multicore CPUs. For the *New* code, we use the same -fopenmp flag as the *Original*
code, as it is also used to enable automatic parallelization of DC loops. The *Experimental* code also uses the same -fopenmp flag. However, as the documentation
states that DC reduction loops are not supported, we do not expect ifort to parallelize them, and rather run them in serial (although as will be shown, the current
compiler version parallelizes the loops anyways, resulting in incorrect results).

4   Results

Here we show timing results for all chosen compilers, code versions, and hardware
(where supported). Key questions we address are: 1) do the compilers that support GPU-acceleration with directives also support it using DC? 2) does replacing
directives with DC lose CPU multicore parallelism? (i.e. do the compilers support
DC for CPU multicore?) 3) for compiler-hardware combinations that support parallelizing DC, how does the performance compare to the baseline directive-based
code? We first report results for the *New* code compared to the *Original* code for
each compiler and hardware type, and afterwards discuss results for the *Experimental* code.

For each configuration, we run the test case of Sect. 2.2, and use the Linux
program time to record three times: real, user, and system. The real time is the
wall clock time the code took to run. The user time is the sum of all thread times, or
how much total CPU computation time was spent. Using multiple threads should
result in a lower real time, but a (much) higher user time. The system time is the
operating system overhead, which can include CPU-GPU data transfer, as well as
other overheads. All reported timings are averaged over 10 runs.

4.1   Results Using nvfortran

The results for the *Original* and *New* code run on the GPU with nvfortran are shown in Table 5. The time difference between the *Original* code and the *New* code is less than 2%, and the standard deviation over the 10 runs is around ±0.1s for both. The slight increase in run time for the *New* code is possibly due to its use of unified memory, which can be less efficient than manually managing the GPU-CPU memory as is done through OpenACC data directives in the *Original* code. This result does not achieve a full replacement of directives with DC since not all directives were replaced in the *New* code. However, the vast majority of them were, with only a few remaining directives on the reduction loops, showing great progress in replacing directives.

Table 5. GPU timing results with nvfortran. Both runs used the additional compiler flag -gpu=cc80,cuda11.4

Code	Compiler flags	real (s)	user (s)	system (s)
Original	-acc=gpu	35.07	34.46	0.59
New	-acc=gpu -stdpar=gpu	35.67	35.01	0.54

To ensure that we did not loose CPU multicore parallelism, we show the CPU results in Table 6. We see that, like in the GPU case, replacing directives with DC yields similar runtimes to the original code. Here, the *New* code with DC runs around 3% faster than the *Original* code, but both are within the standard deviation (±15s) of the 10 runs. Therefore, there is no loss of CPU portability when using DC with nvfortran for our mini-app.

Table 6. CPU timing results with nvfortran

Code	Compiler flags	real (s)	user (s)	system (s)
Serial		1284.59	1272.45	0.22
Original	-acc=multicore	224.18	26214.96	1965.06
New	-acc=multicore -stdpar=multicore	219.57	25638.37	1889.20

4.2   Results Using gfortran

The result for the *Original* code run on the GPU with gfortran is shown in Table 5. Unlike nvfortran, gfortran does not support GPU-acceleration using DC, nor

Table 7. GPU timing results with gfortran.

Code	Compiler flags	real (s)	user (s)	system (s)
Original	-fopenacc -foffload=nvptx-none -fopenacc-dim=::128	49.52	48.90	0.54
New	No Support	-	-	-

is there auto parallelization support for GPU offloading. Therefore, replacing the directives with DC currently breaks support for GPU-acceleration with gfortran. For NVIDIA GPUs, this is not a prohibitive limitation since the nvfortran compiler is freely available. However, for other accelerators (namely AMD GPUs), this loss of support may rule out using DC at this time.

Unlike for GPU-acceleration, CPU multi-core parallelism with gfortran is not lost with DC, even though there is no direct support for DC parallelization. In Table 8, we show the CPU timing results of the *Original* and *New* codes. We see that the performance difference between the codes is ∼10%, within the standard deviations of the 10 runs ($\pm 13s$ for the *Original* and $\pm 18s$ for the *New* code). The *New* code is also able to be parallelized because gfortran treats DC loops as regular do loops, which are parallelized using the auto parallelization feature. However, the loops in diffuse are fairly simple. In other codes, the auto parallelization may not be able to handle more complex loops, that could otherwise be parallelized using directives. Therefore, the result here should be viewed with caution. Note also that the auto parallelization feature works the same on our code with regular do loops as it does with DC loops (i.e. it would even parallelize the *Serial* code version).

Table 8. CPU timing results with gfortran

Code	Compiler flags	real (s)	user (s)	system (s)
Serial		1308.75	1296.74	0.16
Original	-fopenmp	191.90	24117.72	8.02
New	-fopenmp -ftree-parallelize-loops=128	212.64	26588.59	8.65

The thread control for the *New* code is unique. Since the OpenMP directives are still on the reduction loops, while the remaining loops use DC with no directives, the number of CPU threads used for the reductions is set by the standard OMP_NUM_THREADS environment variable, while that used by the DC loops is controlled by the compiler flag value -ftree-parallelize-loops=<N>. This complicates the thread control, and also removes run-time thread control.

4.3   Results Using `ifort`

As mentioned in the introduction, the Intel OpenAPI Toolkit does not currently support GPU-acceleration using DC loops, but there are plans for support in the future. Therefore, here we focus on DC compatibility with multi-core CPU parallelism. In Table 9, we show the timing results for the *Original* and *New* codes. We see that replacing directives with DC still allows for multi-core CPU parallelism, and surprisingly exhibits a nearly 10% improvement in performance. The standard deviation of the 10 runs was roughly $\pm 8s$, so this performance increase is significant. It may be attributed to more efficient optimizations being available to the compiler when using DC compared to OpenMP directives.

Table 9. CPU timing results with `ifort`.

Code	Compiler flags	real (s)	user (s)	system (s)
Serial		1318.60	1306.27	0.18
Original	`-fopenmp`	194.86	24213.11	320.53
New	`-fopenmp`	178.29	21888.21	280.65

Since the implementation of DC parallelism is connected to OpenMP (as indicated by the use of the `-fopenmp` flag), the number of threads remains controlled by the standard environment variable `OMP_NUM_THREADS` (or optionally at compile time with `-par-num-threads=<N>` which overrides `OMP_NUM_THREADS`).

4.4   Experimental Results

As mentioned in Sect. 3.2, the current Fortran standard does not have a way to indicate to the compiler that a DC loop requires reduction or atomic operations. However some compilers have implemented code analysis methods to automatically detect and implement such operations. Therefore, the *Experimental* code, which represents the ideal scenario of replacing all directives with DC loops, may work with some compilers.

Using `nvfortran`, we found that the code parallelized and ran correctly on both the GPU and CPU. It appears `nvfortran` detects the reductions and implements them correctly for our code. The run times are shown in Table 10. They are nearly

Table 10. GPU and CPU timing results for the *Experimental* code with `nvfortran`.

Code	CPU/GPU	Compiler flag	real (s)	user (s)	system (s)
Experimental	GPU	`-stdpar=gpu` `-gpu=cc80,cuda11.4`	35.63	35.01	0.53
Experimental	CPU	`-stdpar=multicore`	219.21	25654.35	1906.40

identical to those of the *New* code shown in Tables 5 and 6 which is expected since only a few small loops used directives for reductions in the *New* code. This means that for `diffuse`, we can use DC to fully eliminate all directives and not lose any CPU or GPU performance with `nvfortran`. We reiterate that more complicated codes may not yet work with zero directives for a variety of reasons including not detecting complicated reduction or atomic operations, not being compatible with in-lined function calls, and, for GPU-acceleration, not supporting automatic memory management with static arrays.

For `gfortran`, we only test the code on the CPU since there is no support for DC GPU-offloading. In this case, the *Experimental* code ran correctly, implying the auto-parallelization done by the compiler was able to detect the reductions and parallelize them. The run time is shown in Table 11 and is roughly 10% slower comparable to the run time of the *New* code in Table 8. However, the times are nearly within the standard deviation of the 10 runs ($\pm 18s$).

Table 11. CPU timing results for the *Experimental* code with `gfortran`.

Code	Compiler flags	real (s)	user (s)	system (s)
Experimental	`-ftree-parallelize-loops=128`	236.28	29565.01	10.08

Using `ifort`, the *Experimental* code compiled and ran, but did not give the correct results. This is because `ifort` does not support implicit reductions of DC loops, yet parallelized the loop anyways when we used the `-fopenmp` flag, Therefore, the resulting inherent race conditions produced incorrect results.

5   Discussion

In this paper, we have used a mini-app code to explore the current status of replacing do loops using directives with `do concurrent` (DC) loops for accelerated computing. The original code used OpenACC for GPU-acceleration when compiled with `gfortran` or `nvfortran`, and OpenMP for multi-core CPU parallelism when compiled with `gfortran`, `nvfortran`, or `ifort`. We modified the code to replace the directives with DC and used a test case to explore the resulting compatibility, portability, and performance, all with the newest available versions of the compilers.

Compatibility: We found that only `nvfortran` currently supports GPU acceleration with DC, and therefore replacing the directives removed GPU support when using `gfortran`. Since `nvfortran` is freely available, this is not an insurmountable problem when running on NVIDIA GPUs. However, `gfortran` also has AMD (and possible future Intel) GPU support, making this an important consideration. The `ifort` compiler does not currently support GPU-acceleration with DC, but as Intel has indicated plans to add this support soon, switching from OpenACC directives to DC may increase compatibility (as `ifort` only supports OpenMP GPU offload, not OpenACC).

We also found that the current Fortran specification for DC lacks features that are needed to guarantee correct parallelization of all of our mini-app's parallelizable loops (specifically, loops with reductions). Indeed, when `ifort` attempted to parallelize our reduction loops for the CPU, it resulted in incorrect results. In contrast, the `nvfortran` compiler has implicit reduction detection of DC loops, allowing us to replace all directives with DC. The next release of the Fortran standard (202x) will include an explicit 'reduce' clause on DC, which, when implemented, should alleviate this issue.

Another compatibility concern is that we currently use OpenACC directives to manually control GPU-CPU memory management, and removing these could cause extreme loss of performance. In the case of `nvfortran`, since it automatically activates its unified memory management feature when compiling with DC GPU-acceleration, this issue is avoided. However, unified memory is limited to allocatable arrays, so static arrays may still require data management directives.

Using cutting-edge language and compiler features have a risk of breaking backward compatibility with older compilers. In this paper we used the most recent versions of the compilers we could for the best support, but on some systems this is not always available. Container frameworks like Singularity/Apptainer (as used here) can help mitigate this issue, however the frameworks are also not always available on all systems, and can sometimes be complicated to use for large scale simulations.

Portability: A key consideration in replacing directives with DC for GPU acceleration was to see if, by doing so, we still maintain CPU multi-core parallelism (that we originally used OpenMP directives to achieve). We found that `nvfortran` and `ifort` compilers directly support DC for multi-core CPU parallelism, while `ifort` requires directives on loops with reductions for correctness. With `gfortran`, while there is no direct support for DC parallelism, the loops can still be parallelized using `gfortran`'s auto parallelization feature. With this feature, even reduction DC loops are correctly recognized and parallelized. Thus, all three compilers we use are able to keep multi-core CPU parallelism when replacing directives with DC (with `ifort` still requiring some on reduction loops).

Performance: Replacing directives with DC allows much cleaner looking code and robustness due to being part of the standard language. However, this is only worth while if it also results in acceptable performance. Through our timings, we found that in both the GPU and CPU cases, the performance of the code after replacing directives with DC was comparable to that of the original directive-based code, with some configurations improving performance slightly, and in others, decreasing slightly. For GPU runs with DC, `nvfortran`'s unified memory was used, and the resulting performance was comparable to using manual OpenACC data directives. However, more complicated codes may not be as compatible with unified memory and/or may lose some performance using it.

Summary: With `nvfortran`, we were able to remove and replace all directives in our code with DC, and achieve efficient CPU and GPU parallelism. However, this relied on specific features of nvfortran including implicitly detecting reductions and the use of unified managed memory. In order to maintain cross compiler compatibility, we can continue to use OpenACC/OpenMP directives for reductions and data movement until equivalent standard language features are written and widely supported. Even with the remaining directives, using DC has a large benefit, as the number of directives is decreased dramatically.

Can Fortran's do concurrent replace directives for accelerated computing? With nvfortran and NVIDIA GPUs, for some codes (such as ours) the answer is yes, and with no (or minimal) loss of performance. With upcoming language features and compiler implementations, more complicated codes may also eventually be parallelized without directives, and do so with support across multiple compiler and hardware vendors.

Appendix

Singularity/Apptainer containers: In order to test the latest compilers and to simplify setup of our library dependencies, we utilized Singularity/Apptainer containers. These containers allow one to run software in a containerized environment on any compatible system using only the container file.

Container setup: The containers were straight forward to setup and use for our timings. Two methods were used to create them. For nvfortran and ifort, a docker image of NVIDIA HPC SDK or Intel OneAPI HPC Toolkit was used to create a sandbox. For gfortran, a similar sandbox with Ubuntu 21.04 was created and then gfortran was installed with the apt-get command. Once the sandboxes were created, the dependent libraries were installed. A sandbox is treated like a virtual machine, allowing us to edit and install new software into the container (note this requires sudo privileges). Once all the needed software is installed, the sandbox is converted to a .sif file which can be copied and run (without sudo privileges) on any other compatible machine with Singularity/Apptainer installed, but it can no longer be edited. However, the container is able to modify files outside itself, allowing us to compile and run the test cases. For GPU-accelerated runs, a special flag is needed when running the container depending on the vendor of GPU. For NVIDIA GPUs, the flag is --nv, while for AMD GPUs, the flag is --rocm. For more details on Singularity/Apptainer containers, see Ref. [7].

Container performance tests: Using containers can sometimes cause performance overhead. To ensure that using the Singularity/Apptainer containers does not cause significant overhead in our case, we ran two test cases on both a bare metal setup and with a container with the same compiler version (in this case gfortran 10.2). Table 12 shows timings of the test run using both the *Original* and *Serial* codes described in Sect. 3.2. We see that the runs using the container perform nearly identical to those run on bare metal, allowing us to confidently use the containers for the runs in the paper.

Table 12. Timing results on a Bridges2 CPU compute node using `gfortran` 10.2 bare metal and form within a Singularity Container

Code	Run method	real (s)	user (s)	system (s)
Serial	Bare Metal	1306.10	1294.30	0.154
	Singularity	1300.43	1287.50	0.168
Original	Bare Metal	164.87	20782.32	5.935
	Singularity	165.27	20777.85	7.248

Reproducibility package: The results in this paper can be reproduced using our reproducibility package hosted publicly at Ref. [9] and on our website[16]. The package contains three Singularity/Apptainer containers (for `gfortran`, `nvfortran`, and `ifort`), as well as all code versions, compiler options, and test cases. The package requires minimal customization (only specifying hardware-specific compiler options) of the main script, which can then be used to automatically run either all, or a subset, of runs from the paper. See the documentation in the package for more details. A reference solution is also provided for validation. Note that runs using GPU-acceleration require having an NVIDIA GPU with compatible drivers installed on the system.

6   Artifact Availability Statement

Summary of the Experiments Reported

Timings were performed on the various mini-app versions on the CPU and GPU using singularity containers. These versions represented different levels of replacing OpenACC and OpenMP directives with do concurrent loops. Each version was tested with the compilers gfortran, nvfortran, and ifort. The compilers were loaded in a singularity container, and the codes were executed through these singularity containers. For each code and compiler version, 10 runs were carried out in order to get an average run time and standard deviation.

Artifact Availability

Software Artifact Availability: All author-created software artifacts are maintained in a public repository under an OSI-approved license.

Hardware Artifact Availability: There are no author-created hardware artifacts.

Data Artifact Availability: All author-created data artifacts are maintained in a public repository under an OSI-approved license.

---

[16] www.predsci.com/papers/dc.

Proprietary Artifacts: No author-created artifacts are proprietary.

List of URLs and/or DOIs where artifacts are available:

```
10.5281/zenodo.5253520
http://www.predsci.com/papers/dc
```

References

1. Balarac, G., et al.: AVBP and YALES2 portability, tuning and scalability on AMD EPYC 7002 Rome processors (2020)
2. Caplan, R.M., Downs, C., Linker, J.: Preparing photospheric magnetic field measurements for use in coronal and heliospheric models. In: AGU Fall Meeting Abstracts, vol. 2019, pp. SH43E–3389 December (2019)
3. Caplan, R.M., Mikić, Z., Linker, J.A., Lionello, R.: Advancing parabolic operators in thermodynamic MHD models: explicit super time-stepping versus implicit schemes with krylov solvers. J. Phys. Conf. Series **837**, 012016 (2017). https://doi.org/10.1088/1742-6596/837/1/012016
4. Caplan, R.M., Downs, C., Linker, J.A., Mikic, Z.: Variations in finite-difference potential fields. Astrophys. J. **915**(1), 44 (2021). https://doi.org/10.3847/1538-4357/abfd2f
5. Chandrasekaran, S., Juckeland, G.: OpenACC for Programmers: Concepts and Strategies. Addison-Wesley Professional (2017)
6. David Olsen, Graham Lopez, B.A.L.: Accelerating standard C++ with GPUs using stdpar (2021).https://developer.nvidia.com/blog/accelerating-standard-c-with-gpus-using-stdpar/
7. Kurtzer, G.M., Sochat, V., Bauer, M.W.: Singularity: scientific containers for mobility of compute. PLOS ONE **12**(5), e0177459 (2017). https://doi.org/10.1371/journal.pone.0177459
8. Meyer, C.D., Balsara, D.S., Aslam, T.D.: A stabilized Runge-Kutta-Legendre method for explicit super-time-stepping of parabolic and mixed equations. J. Comput. Phys. **257**, 594–626 (2014). https://doi.org/10.1016/j.jcp.2013.08.021
9. Mikic, Z., Caplan, R.M., Linker, J.A., Stulajter, M.: Reproducibility package for running the DIFFUSE test cases from "Can Fortran's 'do concurrent' replace directives for accelerated computing" (2021). https://doi.org/10.5281/zenodo.5253520
10. Ozen, G., Lopez, G.: Accelerating Fortran do concurrent with GPUs and the NVIDIA HPC SDK (2020). https://developer.nvidia.com/blog/accelerating-standard-c-with-gpus-using-stdpar/
11. Van der Pas, R., Stotzer, E., Terboven, C.: Using OpenMP The Next Step: Affinity. Tasking, and SIMD. MIT press, Accelerators (2017)
12. Towns, J., Cockerill, T., Dahan, M., Foster, I., Gaither, K., Grimshaw, A., Hazlewood, V., Lathrop, S., Lifka, D., Peterson, G.D., Roskies, R., Scott, J.R., Wilkins-Diehr, N.: XSEDE: accelerating scientific discovery. Comput. Sci. Eng. **16**(5), 62–74 (2014). https://doi.org/10.1109/mcse.2014.80
13. Xinman Tian, Kari Qi, M.L.: Practical examples of OpenMP offload to GPUs (2021).https://techdecoded.intel.io/essentials/3-quick-practical-examples-of-openmp-offload-to-gpus/

Achieving Near-Native Runtime Performance and Cross-Platform Performance Portability for Random Number Generation Through SYCL Interoperability

Vincent R. Pascuzzi[1]([✉])[iD] and Mehdi Goli[2][iD]

[1] Brookhaven National Laboratory, Upton, NY 11973, USA
pascuzzi@bnl.gov
[2] Codeplay Software Ltd., Edinburgh EH3 9DR, UK
mehdi.goli@codeplay.com

Abstract. High-performance computing (HPC) is a major driver accelerating scientific research and discovery, from quantum simulations to medical therapeutics. While the increasing availability of HPC resources is in many cases pivotal to successful science, even the largest collaborations lack the computational expertise required for maximal exploitation of current hardware capabilities. The need to maintain multiple platform-specific codebases further complicates matters, potentially adding constraints on machines that can be utilized. Fortunately, numerous programming models are under development that aim to facilitate portable codes for heterogeneous computing. One in particular is SYCL, an open standard, C++-based single-source programming paradigm. Among the new features available in the most recent specification, SYCL 2020, is interoperability, a mechanism through which applications and third-party libraries coordinate sharing data and execute collaboratively. In this paper, we leverage the SYCL programming model to demonstrate cross-platform performance portability across heterogeneous resources. We detail our NVIDIA and AMD random number generator extensions to the oneMKL open-source interfaces library. Performance portability is measured relative to platform-specific baseline applications executed on four major hardware platforms using two different compilers supporting SYCL. The utility of our extensions are exemplified in a real-world setting via a high-energy physics simulation application. We show the performance of implementations that capitalize on SYCL interoperability are at par with native implementations, attesting to the cross-platform performance portability of a SYCL-based approach to scientific codes.

Keywords: performance portability · HPC · SYCL · random number generators · high energy physics · simulation

© Springer Nature Switzerland AG 2022
S. Bhalachandra et al. (Eds.): WACCPD 2021, LNCS 13194, pp. 22–45, 2022.
https://doi.org/10.1007/978-3-030-97759-7_2

1   Introduction

The proliferation of heterogeneous platforms in high performance computing (HPC) is providing scientists and researchers opportunities to solve some of the world's most important and complex problems. Coalescing central processing units (CPU), co-processors, graphics processing units (GPU) and other hardware accelerators with high-throughput inter-node networking capabilities has driven science and artificial intelligence through insurmountable computational power. Industry continues to innovate in the design and development of increasingly performant architectures and platforms, with each vendor typically commercializing a myriad of proprietary libraries optimized for their specific hardware. What this means for physicists and other domain scientists is that their codes need to be translated, or ported, to multiple languages, or adapted to some specific programming model for best performance. While this could be a useful and instructive exercise for some, many are often burdened by their limited numbers of developers that can develop such codes. Fortunately, as a result of the numerous architectures and platforms, collaborative groups within academia, national laboratories and even industry are developing portability layers atop common languages that aim to target a variety of vendor hardware. Such examples include Kokkos [21] (Sandia National Laboratory, USA), RAJA [25] (Lawrence Livermore National Laboratory, USA) and SYCL [12] (Khronos Group).

Mathematical libraries are crucial to the development of scientific codes. For instance, the use of random numbers in scientific applications, in particular high energy physics (HEP) software, is almost ubiquitous [26]. For example, HEP experiments typically have a number of steps that are required as part of their Monte Carlo (MC) production: event generation, simulation, digitization and reconstruction. In the first step, an MC event generator [17] produces the outgoing particles and their four-vectors given some physical process. Here, random numbers are used, *e.g.*, to sample initial state kinematics and evaluate cross sections. Simulation software, *e.g.*, Geant4 [15] and FastCaloSim [20,31] from the ATLAS Experiment [14], require large quantities of random numbers for sampling particle energies and secondary production kinematics, and digitization requires detector readout emulation, among others. With the rise of machine learning, random number production is required even at the analysis level [22].

1.1   Contribution

The focus of this paper is to evaluate the cross-platform performance portability of SYCL's interoperability functionality using various closed-source vendor random number generation APIs within a single library, and analyze the performance of our implementation in both artificial and real-world applications.

To achieve this, we have:

- integrated AMD and NVIDIA random number generators (RNG) within the oneMKL open-source interfaces library by leveraging existing hipRAND and cuRAND libraries, to target these HPC hardware from these vendors from a single API via SYCL interoperability;

– evaluated the performance portability of the API on Intel and AMD CPUs, and Intel, AMD and NVIDIA GPUs to investigate the performance overhead of the abstraction layer introduced by the SYCL API;
– integrated our RNG implementations into FastCaloSim to further investigate the applicability of the proposed solution on an existing real-world application for high-energy physics calorimeter simulations, which currently relies on separate implementations based on vendor-dependent libraries; and
– analyzed the cross-platform performance portability by comparing the SYCL-based implementation of FastCaloSim to the original C++-based and CUDA codes, which use native vendor-dependent RNGs, to investigate possible performance overheads associated with SYCL interoperability.

Our work utilizes Data Parallel C++ (DPC++) [6] and hipSYCL [16], two different existing LLVM-based SYCL compilers, capable of providing plug-in interfaces for CUDA and HIP support as part of SYCL 2020 features that enable developers to target NVIDIA and AMD GPUs, respectively.

The rest of this paper is organized as follows. Section 2 discusses existing parallel programming models and libraries providing functionalities used in scientific applications, along with our proposed solution to target the cross-platform portability issue. Section 3 briefly introduces the SYCL programming model used in this work. In Sect. 4, we discuss more technically the aspects and differences between the cuRAND and hipRAND APIs, and also detail the implementation of our work. Benchmark applications are described in Sect. 5 and performance portability in Sect. 6. The results of our studies are presented in Sect. 7. Lastly, Sect. 8 summarizes our work and suggests potential extensions and improvements for future developments.

2   Related Work

2.1   Parallel Programming Frameworks

Parallelism across a variety of hardware can be provided through a number different parallel frameworks, each having a different approach and programming style. Typically written in C or C++, each framework provides different variations on the language, allowing programmers to specify the task parallel patterns.

Introduced by Intel, Thread Building Blocks (TBB) [30] provides a C++-based template library supporting parallel programming on multi-core processors. TBB only support parallelism on CPUs, hence, parallel applications dependent on TBB cannot be directly ported to GPUs or any other accelerator-based platform.

NVIDIA's CUDA [9] API is a C/C++-based low-level parallel programming framework exclusively for NVIDIA GPUs. Its support of C++-based template meta programming features enables CUDA to provide performance portability across various NVIDIA devices and architectures, however, its lack of portability

across other vendor hardware can be a barrier for research groups with access
to non-NVIDIA resources.

OpenCL [33], from the Khronos Group, is an open-standard cross-platform
framework supported by various vendors and hardware platforms However, its
low-level C-based interface and lack of support by some vendors could hinder
the development of performance portability on various hardware. Also from the
Khronos Group is SYCL [12], an open-standard C++-based programming model
that facilitates the parallel programming on heterogeneous platforms. SYCL provides a single-source abstraction layer enabling developers to write both host-
side and kernel code in the same file. Employing C++-based template programming, developers can leverage higher level programming features when writing
accelerator-enabled applications, having the ability to integrate the native acceleration API, when needed, by using the different interoperability interfaces provided.

The Kokkos [21] and RAJA [25] abstraction layers expose a set of C++-
based parallel patterns to facilitate operations such as parallel loop execution,
reorder, aggregation, tiling, loop partitioning and kernel transformation. They
provide C++-based portable APIs for users to alleviate the difficulty of writing specialized code for each system. The APIs can be mapped onto a specific
backend—including OpenMP, CUDA, and more recently SYCL—at runtime to
provide portability across various architectures.

2.2 Linear Algebra Libraries

There are several vendor-specific libraries which provide highly optimized linear
algebra routines for specific hardware platforms. The ARM Compute Library [13]
provides a set of optimized functions for linear algebra and machine learning optimized for ARM devices. Intel provides MKL [5] for its linear algebra subroutines
for accelerating BLAS, LAPACK and RNG routines targeting Intel chips, and
NVIDIA provides a wide ecosystem of closed source libraries for linear algebra
operations, including cuBLAS [8] for BLAS routines, cuRAND [10] for RNG and
cuSPARSE [11] for sparse linear algebra. AMD offers a set of hipBLAS [1] and
hipRAND [2] libraries atop the ROCm platform, which provide linear algebra
routines for AMD GPUs. Each of these libraries is optimized specifically for particular hardware architectures, and therefore do not provide portability across
vendor hardware.

oneMKL [7] is an community-driven open-source interface library developed
using the SYCL programming model, providing linear algebra and RNG functionalities used in various domains such as high-performance computing, artificial intelligence and other scientific domains. The front-end SYCL-based interface could be mapped to the vendor-optimized backend implementations either
via direct SYCL kernel implementations or SYCL interoperability using built-in
vendor libraries to target various hardware backends. Currently, oneMKL supports BLAS interfaces with vendor-optimized backend implementations for Intel
GPU and CPU, CUDA GPUs and RNG interfaces which wrap the optimized
Intel routines targeting x86 architectures and Intel GPUs.

2.3   The Proposed Approach

There are numerous highly-optimized libraries implemented for different device-specific parallel frameworks targeting different hardware architectures and platforms. Several parallel frameworks provide parallel models which hide the memory hierarchies and execution policies on different hardware. This can be due to a lack of a common language to abstract away the memory and execution models from various heterogeneous devices, hence, leaving cross-platform performance portability of high-level applications a challenging issue and an active area of research. Recent work in adopting SYCL [18,19,32] as the unifying programming model has shown to be a viable approach for developing cross-platform performance portable solutions targeting various hardware architectures while sharing the same interface. More specifically, SYCL interoperability with built-in kernels enables vendors to use a common unifying interface, to "glue-in" their optimized hardware-specific libraries.

In this paper, we leverage the SYCL programming model and interoperability to enable cross-platform performance portable random number generator targeting major HPC hardware, including NVIDIA and AMD GPUs. The proposed solution has been integrated into the oneMKL open-source interfaces library as additional backends targeting these vendors, extending the library's portability and offering nearly native performance. The applicability of the proposed approach was further studied in a high-energy physics calorimeter simulation software to evaluate the performance of the proposed abstraction method on a real-world scientific application.

3   SYCL Overview

SYCL is an open-standard C++-based programming model that facilitates parallel programming on heterogeneous platforms. It provides a single source programming model, enabling developers to write both host-side and kernel code in the same file. Employing C++-based template programming, developers can leverage higher-level programming features when developing accelerator-enabled applications. Developers also have the ability to integrate the native acceleration API, when needed, by using the different interoperability interfaces provided by SYCL.

A SYCL application is structured in three code scopes that control the flow, as well as the construction and lifetimes of the various objects used within it.

- *Application scope*: all code outside of a command group scope
- *Command group scope*: specifies a unit of work that is comprised of a kernel function and data accessors
- *Kernel scope*: specifies a single kernel function to interface with native objects and is executed on the device

To execute a SYCL kernel on an accelerator device, *command groups* containing the kernel must be submitted to a SYCL queue. When a command group is submitted to a queue, the SYCL runtime system tracks data dependencies and creates (expands) a new (existing) dependency graph—a directed acyclic graph (DAG)—to orchestrate kernel executions. Once the dependency graph is created, the correct ordering of kernel execution on any available device is guaranteed by the SYCL runtime system via a set of rules defined for dependency checking[1].

Interoperability is enabled via the aforementioned low-level APIs by facilitating the SYCL runtime system's interaction with native objects for the supported backends [12,23].

SYCL interoperating with existing native objects is supported by either `host_task` or `interop_task` interfaces inside the command group scope. When using the `interop_task` interface, the SYCL runtime system injects a task into the runtime DAG that will execute from the host, but ensures dependencies are satisfied on the device. This allows code within a kernel scope to be written as though it were running directly at the low-level API on the host, but produces side-effects on the device, *e.g.*, external API or library function calls.

There are several implementations of SYCL API available including ComputeCpp [3] that currently supports the SYCL 1.2.1 specification, DPC++ and hipSYCL which incorporate SYCL 2020 features, such as unified shared memory (USM), and triSYCL [24] which provides SYCL supports for FPGAs.

4 SYCL-Based RNG Implementations of NVIDIA and AMD GPUs in oneMKL

4.1 Technical Aspects

The integration of third-party RNG backends within oneMKL depends primarily on compiler support for (a) SYCL 2020 interoperability and (b) generating the specific intermediate representation for a given architecture's source code. Hence, to enable RNG on NVIDIA and AMD GPUs, one requires SYCL compilers supporting parallel thread (PTX) and Radeon Open Compute (ROCm) execution instruction set architectures which are used in the CUDA and AMD programming environment, respectively. At present, PTX support is available in Intel's open-source LLVM project, and the ROCm backend is supported by the hipSYCL LLVM project.

The oneMKL interface library provides both buffer and USM API implementations for memory management. Buffers are encapsulating objects which hide the details of pointer-based memory management. They provide a simple yet powerful way for the SYCL runtime system to handle data dependencies between kernels, both on the host and device, when building the data-flow DAG. The USM API gives a more traditional pointer-based approach, *e.g.*, memory allocations performed with `malloc` and `malloc_device`, familiar to those accustomed to C++ and CUDA. However, unlike buffers, the SYCL runtime system cannot generate the data dependency graph from USM alone, and so it is the user's responsibility to ensure dependencies are met. The ability for SYCL to

---

[1] This is not the case when using unified shared memory, as explained later.

internally satisfy buffer-based data dependencies is beneficial in cases when quick prototyping is, to first order, more important than optimizing. Figure 1 represents the architectural view of the cuRAND and hipRAND integration for each scope in the SYCL programming model for both buffer-based approach and USM-based approaches.

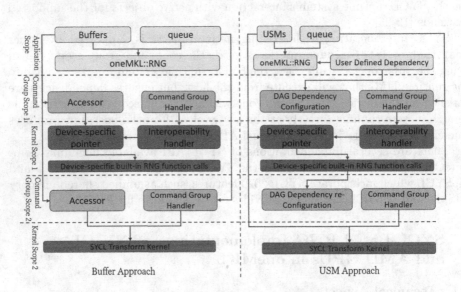

Fig. 1. Architectural view of device-specific RNG kernels integration in oneMKL for both cuRAND and hipRAND on different scopes in SYCL programming model using both buffer and USM approach.

The oneMKL library currently contains implementations for Philox- and MRG-based generators for ×86 and Intel GPUs. In oneMKL, each engine class comprises 36 high-level `generate` function templates—18 per buffer and USM API—with template parameters to specify a distribution and output types. In addition to having the ability to specify distribution properties, *e.g.*, mean, standard deviation for Gaussian distributions, custom ranges on the generated numbers can also be specified. This is in sharp contrast to the lower level interfaces provided by cuRAND or hipRAND; generation of random numbers is performed using functions with fixed types, and there is no concept of a "range", and it is therefore left to the user to post-process the generated numbers. For example, `curandGenerateNormal` will output a sequence of normally-distributed pseudo-random numbers in $[0, 1)$ and there is no API functionality to transform the range. As such, native cuRAND and hipRAND support generation of strictly positive-valued numbers.

Lastly, whereas oneMKL provides copy-constructors and constructors for setting seed initializer lists for multiple sequences, cuRAND and hipRAND do not. The oneMKL library also supports inverse cumulative distribution function (ICDF) methods for pseudorandom number generation, while such methods are available only for quasirandom number generators in the cuRAND and hipRAND API.

4.2   Native cuRAND and hipRAND flow

Generation of random numbers with cuRAND and hipRAND host APIs in native applications typically has the following workflow:

1. the creation of a generator of a desired type;
2. setting generator options, *e.g.*, seed, offset, *etc.*;
3. allocation of memory on the device using {cuda, hip}Malloc;
4. generation of the random numbers using a generation function, *e.g.*, {cu, hip}randGenerate; and
5. clean up by calling the generator destructor {cu, hip}randDestroyGenerator and {cuda, hip}Free.

In addition, a user may wish to use the generated numbers on the host, in which case host memory must also be allocated and data transferred between devices.

4.3   Implementation of cuRAND and hipRAND in oneMKL

Our implementation of cuRAND and hipRAND libraries within oneMKL follows closely the procedure outlined in Sect. 4.2. We also include additional *range transformation* kernels for specifying the output sequence of random numbers, a feature not available in the cuRAND and hipRAND APIs.

Each generator class comprises a native xrandGenerator_t object, where xrand could be either of curand or hiprand. Class constructors create the generator via a native xrandCreateGenerator API call and sets the seed for generation of the output sequence with xrandSetPseudoRandomGeneratorSeed; due to limitations of the cuRAND and hipRAND host API, our implementation does not support copy-construction or seed initializer lists. Of the total 36 generate functions available in oneMKL, 20 are supported by our cuRAND and hipRAND backends as the remaining 16 use ICDF methods (see Sect. 4.1). Each generate function in the cuRAND and hipRAND backends have the same signature as the corresponding ×86 and Intel GPU function to facilitate "pointer-to-implementation".

The buffer and USM API generate function implementations are nearly identical; access to the buffer pointer via a SYCL accessor is needed before retrieving the native CUDA memory.

```
1  virtual inline void generate(
2    const oneapi::mkl::rng::uniform<float, uniform_method::standard>& distr,
3    std::int64_t n, cl::sycl::buffer<float, 1>& r) override {
4    queue_.submit([&](cl::sycl::handler& cgh) {
5      auto acc = r.get_access<cl::sycl::access::mode::read_write>(cgh);
6      cgh.codeplay_host_task([=](cl::sycl::interop_handle ih) {
7        auto r_ptr = reinterpret_cast<float*>(
8          ih.get_native_mem<cl::sycl::backend::cuda>(acc));
9        curandStatus_t status;
10       CURAND_CALL(curandGenerateUniform, status, engine_, r_ptr, n);
11       cudaError_t err;
12       CUDA_CALL(cudaDeviceSynchronize, err);
13     });
14   });
15   range_transform_fp<float>(queue_, distr.a(), distr.b(), n, r);
16 }
```

Listing 1.1. Example code calling functions from the cuRAND library within a SYCL kernel using the buffer API.

```
1  template <typename T>
2  static inline void range_transform_fp(cl::sycl::queue& queue, T a, T b,
3                                         std::int64_t n,
4                                         cl::sycl::buffer<T, 1>& r) {
5    queue.submit([&](cl::sycl::handler& cgh) {
6      auto acc =
7        r.template get_access<cl::sycl::access::mode::read_write>(cgh);
8      cgh.parallel_for(cl::sycl::range<1>(n), [=](cl::sycl::id<1> id) {
9        acc[id] = acc[id] * (b - a) + a;
10     });
11   });
12 }
```

Listing 1.2. Example code of transform function for cuRAND using the buffer API. The function can be used to transform the range of the generated numbers. Its dependencies are detected via the auto-generated runtime DAG graph from SYCL accessors.

As shown in Fig. 1, cuRAND and hipRAND backend integration into the oneMKL open-source interfaces library requires two kernels. The first kernel makes the corresponding xrandGenerate third-party library function call, as per the distribution function template parameter type; Listing 1.1 shows an example kernel for the cuRAND backend using the buffer API. A second kernel is required to adjust the range of the generated numbers, altering the output sequence as required. As this is not a native functionality in the cuRAND and hipRAND APIs, we implemented this it as a SYCL kernel. Listing 1.2 gives an example of one such transformation kernel for floating-point data types using the buffer API. It is hardware agnostic: the same code can be compiled for, and executed on, all platforms for which there exists a SYCL compiler. In the command group scope, an accessor is required for the buffer API to track the kernel dependency and memory access within the kernel scope. In this case, the graph dependencies between the two kernels are automatically detected by the SYCL runtime system scheduling thread, tracking the data-flow based on the data access type, *e.g.*, read, write, read_write. The accessor has a read_write access type and is passed as an input with read_write for *in-situ* updates to be made. This forces the transformation kernel to depend on the SYCL interoperability kernel and hence the kernels will be scheduled for execution in this order.

The USM API does not require `accessors` in the command group scope, but does take an additional argument for specifying dependent kernels for subsequent calculations on the data outputted. The dependency is preserved by a direct injection of the `event` object returned by the command group handler to the existing dependency list.

Inside the kernel scope for both buffer and USM APIs, calls to the cuRAND or hipRAND API are made from the host and, if using buffers, the `accessor` is then reinterpreted as native memory—*i.e.*, a raw pointer to be used for cuRAND and hipRAND API calls. The random numbers are then generated by calling the appropriate `xrandGenerate` as per the distribution function template parameter type.

The application scope remains the same as the one proposed in the oneMKL SYCL RNG interface for both buffer and USM API, enabling users to seamlessly execute codes on AMD or NVIDIA GPUs with no code modification whatever.

5   Benchmark Applications

Two benchmark applications were used for performance portability studies, and are detailed below. The SYCL codes were compiled using the `sycl-nightly-20210330` tag of the Intel LLVM open-source DPC++ compiler for targeting CUDA devices and hipSYCL v0.9.0 for AMD GPUs. The applications' native counterparts were compiled with `nvcc` 10.2 and `hipcc` 4.0, respectively, for NVIDIA and AMD targets. Calls to the high-resolution `std::chronos` clock were bootstrapped at different points of program execution to measure the execution time of different routines in the codes.

5.1   Random Number Generation Burner

The first application was designed as an artificial benchmark to stress the hardware used in the experiments by generating a sequence of pseudorandom numbers of a given batch size using a specified API—*i.e.*, CUDA, HIP or SYCL—and platform. We use this simple test as the primary measure of our oneMKL RNG implementations. Having a single application to benchmark all available platforms has a number of advantages, namely, ensuring ease of consistency among the separate target platform APIs, *e.g.*, all memory allocations, and data transfers between host and devices are performed analogously for each API.

The workflow of this benchmark application can be outlined as follows:

1. target platform, API and generator type are chosen at compile-time, specified by `ifdef` directives;
2. target distribution from which to sample, number of iterations and cardinality of the output pseudorandom sequence are specified at runtime; for SYCL targets, buffer or USM API is also specified;

3. host and device memory are allocated, and the generator is constructed and initialized; for SYCL targets, a distribution object is also created as per Step 2 above;
4. pseudorandom output sequence is generated and its range is transformed; and
5. the output sequence is copied from device memory to host memory.

5.2 FastCaloSim

Our second benchmark is a real-world application that aims to solve a real-world problem: rapid production of sufficiently accurate high-energy collider physics simulations[2]. The parameterized calorimeter simulation software, FastCaloSim [31], was developed by the ATLAS Experiment [14] for this reason. The primary ATLAS detector comprises three sub-detectors; from inner radii outward, a silicon-based inner tracking detector; two types of calorimeter technologies consisting of liquid argon or scintillating tiles for measurements of traversing particles' energies; and at the periphery a muon spectrometer. Among these three sub-detectors, the simulation of the calorimeters are the most CPU-intensive due to the complex showering—*i.e.* production of additional particles in particle-material interactions—and stopping of highly energetic particles, predominantly in the liquid argon calorimeters.

The original FastCaloSim codes, written in standard C++, were ported to CUDA and Kokkos [20], and subsequently to SYCL; the three ports were written to be as similar as possible in their kernels and program flow so as to permit comparisons between their execution and runtimes. The SYCL port, largely inspired in its design by the CUDA version, permits execution on AMD, Intel and NVIDIA hardware, whereas the CUDA port permits execution on NVIDIA GPUs exclusively.

We briefly describe the core functionality of FastCaloSim here; for more details on the C++ codes and CUDA port, the reader is referred respectively to [31] and [20]. The detector geometry includes nearly 190,000 detecting elements, $\mathcal{O}(10)$ MB, each of which can record a fraction of a traversing particle's energy. Various parameterization inputs, $\mathcal{O}(1)$ GB, are used for different particles' energy and shower shapes, derived from Geant4 simulations. The detector geometry, about 20 MB of data, is loaded onto the GPU; due to the large file size of the parameterization inputs, only those data required—based on the particle type and kinematics—are transferred during runtime.

The number of calorimeter *hits*—*i.e.* energy deposited by interacting particles in the sensitive elements—depends largely on the physics process being simulated. For a given physics event, the number of secondary particles produced can range from one to $\mathcal{O}(10^4)$, depending on the incident parent particle type, energy and location in the calorimeter. Three uniformly-distributed pseudorandom numbers are required for each hit to sample from the relevant energy distribution, with the minimum set to 200,000 (approximately one per calorimeter cell).

---

[2] Use of proprietary data that cannot be made publicly available.

We consider two different simulation scenarios in our performance measurements. The first is an input sample of 10^3 single-electron events, where each electron carries a kinetic energy of 65 GeV and traverses a small angular region of the calorimeters. An average number of hits from this sample is typically 4000–6500, leading to 12000–19500 random numbers per event. Because only a single particle type is used within a limited region of the detector, this scenario requires only several energy and shower shape parameterizations to be loaded onto the GPU during runtime. The second, more realistic, scenario uses an input of 500 top quark pair ($t\bar{t}$) events. In this simulation, the number of calorimeter hits is roughly 600–800 times greater than the single-electron case, requiring $\mathcal{O}(10^7)$ random numbers in total be generated during simulation. Also, a range of secondary particles are produced with various energies that traverse a range of angular regions of the detector. As such, $t\bar{t}$ simulations require data from 20–30 separate parameterizations that need to be loaded to the GPU during runtime, and thus result in a significant increases in time-to-solution on both CPUs and GPUs.

6   Performance Evaluation

6.1   Performance Portability Metrics

There are numerous definitions of performance portability, e.g., [21,27,28,34]. In this paper, we adopt the definition from [29]: the performance portability $\mathcal{P}$ of an application a that solves a problem p correctly on all platforms in a given set H is given by,

$$\mathcal{P}(a,p;H) = \begin{cases} \dfrac{|H|}{\sum_{i \in H} \dfrac{1}{e_i(a,p)}} & \text{if } i \text{ is supported } \forall_i \in H \\ 0 & \text{otherwise} \end{cases}, \qquad (1)$$

where $e_i(a, p)$ is the *performance efficiency* of a solving p on $i \in H$. We introduce an *application efficiency* metric, being the ratio between the time-to-solution (TTS) measured using our portable, vendor-agnostic (VA) solution to the native, vendor-specific (VS) performance,

$$\text{VAVS} \equiv \frac{TTS_{\text{portable}}}{TTS_{\text{native}}}. \qquad (2)$$

The VAVS metric is useful to identify if runtime overheads are introduced in portability layers which otherwise do not exist in a native API optimized for a specific platform.

6.2   Hardware Specifications

We evaluate performance portability using a variety of AMD, Intel and NVIDIA platforms, ranging from consumer-grade to high-end hardware. This large set of platforms can be subdivided into CPUs and GPUs, as well as the union of the two, and also helps determine the regime in which the use of GPUs is more efficient for solving a given problem, if one exists.

The Intel x86-based platform tested was a Core i7-10875, consisting of 8 physical CPU cores and 16 threads, a base (maximum) clock frequency of 2.30 (5.10) GHz. To benchmark native oneMKL GPU performance, we use the Intel(R) UHD Graphics 630, an integrated GPU (iGPU) that shares the same silicon die as the host CPU described previously. This iGPU has 24 compute units (CU) and base (maximum) frequency of 350 (1200) MHz. Through Intel's unified memory architecture (UMA), the iGPU has a theoretical maximum memory of 24.98 GB, *i.e.*, the total available RAM on the host. The main advantage of UMA is that it enables zero-copy buffer transfers; no buffer copy between the host and iGPU is required since physical memory is shared between them.

We evaluated SYCL interoperability for AMD and NVIDIA GPUs using an MSI Radeon RX Vega 56 and NVIDIA A100. The Radeon is hosted by an Intel Xeon Gold 5220 36-core processor with a base (maximum) clock of 2.2 (3.9) GHz. An AMD CPU and NVIDIA GPU were evaluated using a DGX A100 node, comprising an AMD Rome 7742 64-core processor with a base (maximum) clock frequency of 2.25 (3.4) GHz. The A100 is NVIDIA's latest high-end GPU, with 6912 CUDA cores and peak FP32 (FP64) of 19.5 (9.7) TF. Note that 16 CPU cores and a single A100 of the DGX were used for these studies.

6.3   Software Specifications

The software used for these studies can be found in Table 1. As our work is relevant only for Linux operating systems (OS), all test machines run some flavor of Linux that supports the underlying hardware and software required for our studies. In this table, DPC++ refers to the Intel LLVM compiler nightly tag from March 3, 2021; separate builds of the compiler were used for targeting $\times 86$ platforms and NVIDIA GPUs. The HIP compiler and hipSYCL are based on Clang 12.0.0, and were installed from pre-compiled binaries available from [4].

Our implementations of SYCL-based cuRAND and hipRAND RNGs within oneMKL were compiled into separate libraries for each platform using the respective compiler for the targeted vendor.

7   Results

The RNG burner application was run 100 iterations for each batch size for statistically meaningful measurements. Each test shown in the following was performed with the Philo $\times 4 \times 32 \times 10$ generator to produce uniformly-distributed FP32 pseudorandom numbers in batches between 1–10^8, as per the requirements of our FastCaloSim benchmark application. Unless otherwise specified, all measurements are of the total execution time, which includes generator construction, memory allocation, host-to-device data transfers, generation and postprocessing (*i.e.*, range transformations), synchronisation and finally device-to-

Table 1. Driver and software versions for each platform considered in these studies.

Platform	Driver version	OS and Kernel	Compiler	RNG library
AMD Rome 7742	-	OpenSUSE 15.0 4.12	GNU 8.2.0 DPC++	CLHEP 2.3.4.6 oneMKL
Intel Core i7-1080H	-	Ubuntu 20.04 5.8.18	GNU 8.4.0 DPC++	CLHEP 2.3.4.6 oneMKL
Intel UHD Graphics	21.11.19310	Ubuntu 20.04 5.8.18	DPC++	oneMKL
Radeon RX Vega 56	20.50	CentOS 7 3.10.0	HIP 4.0.0 hipSYCL 0.9.0	hipRAND 4.0.0 oneMKL
NVIDIA A100	450.102.04	OpenSUSE 15.0 4.12	CUDA 10.2.89 DPC++	cuRAND 10.2.89 oneMKL

host data transfer times, as determined by the high-resolution `std::chronos` clock.

Shown in Fig. 2 are plots of the total FP32 generation time for the two x86-based CPUs, as well the integrated GPU, using Philox-based generator for both buffer and USM APIs. In general, little overhead is introduced when using the USM API versus buffers. This is a promising result and, to the authors' knowledge, the first benchmark of the different APIs; it is often more productive for developers to port existing codes to SYCL using USM as this approach is often more familiar to C++ programmers who use dynamic memory allocations in their applications.

Figure 3 shows separately the RNG burner application results between the buffer and USM APIs, and their native counterparts. Again, we observe statistically equivalent performance using either buffers or USM, with a slight overhead at large batch sizes DPC++ USM and the A100 GPU. More importantly, however, is the level of performance achieved by our cross-platform RNG implementation; TTS for both the cuRAND and hipRAND SYCL backend implementations are on par with their native application.

One immediate point of discussion are the differences in TTS between the Radeon oneMKL-based generator application and native application: the oneMKL version shows slightly better performance for small batch sizes. This is understood as being a result of the optimizations within the hipRAND runtime system for its ROCm back-end. Due to the data dependencies among the three kernels—seeding, generation and post-processing—in the test application, call-backs are issued to signal task completion. These call-backs introduce latencies into the application execution that are significant with respect to small-scale kernels. The nearly callback-free hipRAND runtime system therefore offers higher task throughput. As the batch sizes increase to 10^8, the difference in TTS becomes negligible.

To further investigate this discrepancy, we separate each kernel's duration for both the oneMKL and native cuRAND applications; due to technical and soft-

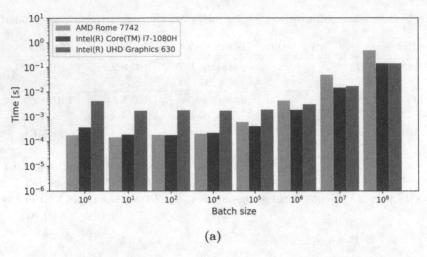

(a)

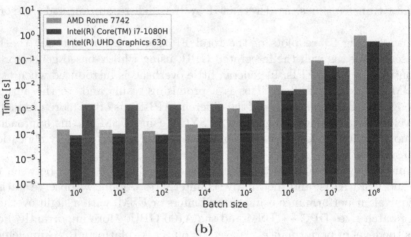

(b)

Fig. 2. Results from the RNG burner test application using the buffer API (a) and USM API (b) for Philo $\times 4 \times 32 \times 10$ generation of uniformly-distributed FP32 pseudorandom numbers.

ware limitations, we were unable to profile the Radeon GPU in the following way. Three kernels in total are profiled: generator seeding, generation and our transformation kernel that post-processes the output sequence to the defined range. Figure 4 shows both the time of each kernel executed and relative occupancy in the RNG burner application using data collected from NVIDIA Nsight Compute 2020.2.1. Comparison between each kernel duration is statistically compatible over a series of ten runs. It can therefore conclude that the discrepancies in Fig. 3 between the Radeon oneMKL and native applications can be attributed to differences between the applications themselves, and not fundamentally to the native library kernel executions. Shown also in Fig. 4(b) are the relative occupancy of

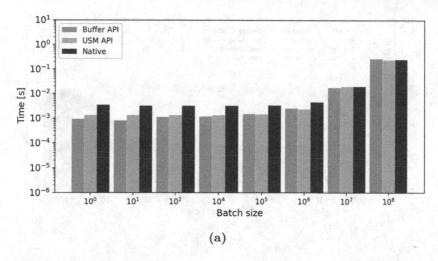

(a)

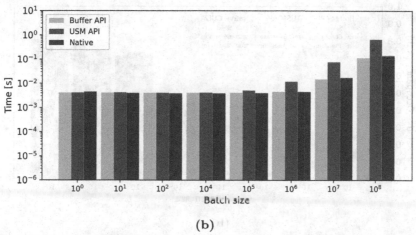

(b)

Fig. 3. Comparisons of the RNG burner test application execution time between SYCL buffer and USM APIs, and their native counterparts running on the MSI Radeon RX Vega 56 (a) and NVIDIA A100 (b). The Philo $\times 4 \times 32 \times 10$ generator was used to produce uniformly-distributed FP32 pseudorandom numbers of different batch sizes.

each kernel for the batch sizes generated. Both cuRAND kernels—seeding and generation—are in all cases statistically equivalent between oneMKL and the native application. It can be seen that, despite the nearly identical kernel duration, the buffer and USM API occupancies have a large increase between 10^2 and 10^4 in batch size compared to the native occupancy. This is because when not explicitly specified, the SYCL runtime system optimizes the number of required block size and threads-per-block, whereas in CUDA these values must be determined by the developer as per the hardware specifications. While in the native version the thread-per-block size is fixed to 256, the SYCL kernel runtime chose

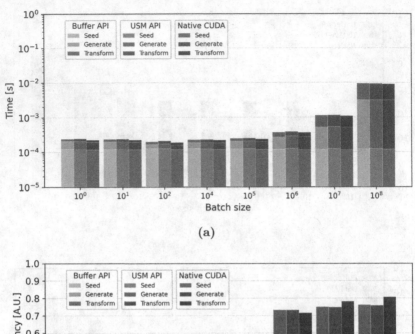

(a)

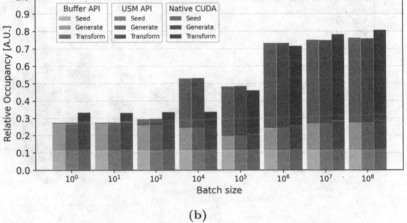

(b)

Fig. 4. Per-kernel total execution time (a) and relative occupancy (b) executed on the NVIDIA A100 with the Philo $\times 4 \times 32 \times 10$ generator producing uniformly-distributed pseudorandom sequences of various batch sizes.

1024 for the NVIDIA A100 GPU. This resulted in the observed differences in kernel occupancy in the native application, as opposed to the SYCL codes for the transform kernel which handle such intricacies at the device level.

Table 2 reports the calculated performance portability of our oneMKL RNG backends using the VAVS metric introduced in Sect. 6. Note that VAVS values closer to unity are representative of greater performance, while smaller values are indicative of poor performance. The data used in calculating the various values of $\mathcal{P}$ are taken from Fig. 4.

Table 2. Calculated performance portability using the VAVS metric.

H	$\mathcal{P}$ buffer	$\mathcal{P}$ USM	$\mathcal{P}$ Mean (buffer+USM)
{Vega 56, A100}	1.070	0.393	0.575
{Vega 56}	0.974	1.076	1.022
{A100}	1.186	0.240	0.400

As reported in Table 2, the performance portability measure in a number of cases is greater than unity. This result is consistent with the performance improvement over the native version observed in Fig. 3 for the buffer API on both AMD and NVIDIA GPUs. Although the interoperability kernel time is the same in both native and SYCL versions (see Fig. 4(a)), the buffer API leverages the SYCL runtime system DAG mechanism and hipSYCL optimizations, improving throughput relative to the native application, particularly for small batch sizes. On the other hand, the DPC++ runtime system scheduler does not perform the same with USM as it does when using buffers. Therefore, the performance drop observed in the USM version in Fig. 3 leads to a reduction in the performance portability metric by ~%40. This behaviour is not observed with hipSYCL.

As a demonstration of cross-platform performance portability in a real-world application, we show in Fig. 5 the average runtime of the FastCaloSim code implementing the proposed SYCL RNG solution across four platforms. Both SYCL and native implementations are shown for each platform, with the exception of the Radeon GPU as no native HIP-based port exists. Ten single-electron and $t\bar{t}$ simulations were run on each platform for reliability of measurements. Where applicable, all measurements made in this study are consistent with those in [20]. The left plot in the figure pertains to the 10,000 single-electron events and the right to the 500 $t\bar{t}$ events (see Sect. 5.2).

In the simpler scenario of single electrons, an approximately 80% reduction in processing time is required on the Vega or A100 GPUs compared to the CPUs considered. However, the overall insufficient use of the full compute capability of the GPUs in this application is made apparent in the more complex topology of $t\bar{t}$ events. This inefficiency is due primarily to the initial strategy in porting FastCaloSim to GPUs; while maximum intra-event parallelism—*i.e.* parallel processing of individual hits within a given event—is met, inter-event parallelism is not implemented in this version of the codes. Future work on the FastCaloSim ports includes event batching to better utilize GPU compute but is beyond the scope of this paper. While the contribution of RNG to the overall runtime of FastCaloSim is small, to investigate SYCL as a portability solution for these codes nevertheless required a SYCL RNG to do so. With cuRAND and hipRAND support added to oneMKL, we can run this prototype application on all major vendors' platforms with no code modifications whatever, and with comparable performance to native codes.

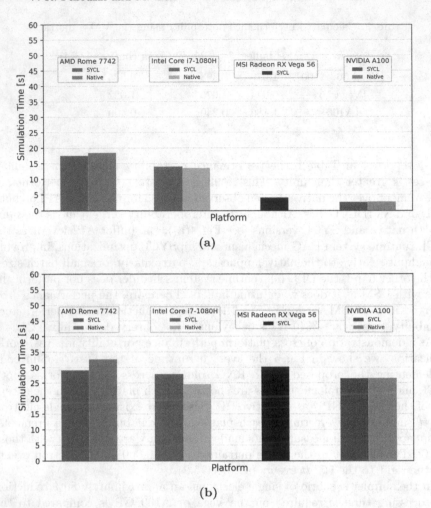

Fig. 5. Total runtimes of FastCaloSim across a range of platforms simulating single-electron events (a) and $t\bar{t}$ events (b).

8   Conclusions and Future Work

In this paper, we detailed our implementations of cuRAND and hipRAND backends into oneMKL, and studied their cross-platform performance portability in two SYCL-based applications using major high performance computing hardware, including x86-based CPUs from AMD and Intel, and AMD, NVIDIA and Intel GPUs. We have shown that utilizing SYCL interoperability enables performance portability of highly-optimized platform-dependent libraries across different hardware architectures. The performance evaluation of our RNG codes carried out in this paper demonstrates little overhead when exploiting vendor-optimized native libraries through interoperability methods.

The applicability of the proposed solution has been evaluated in a parameterized calorimeter simulation software, FastCaloSim, a real-world application consisting of thousands of lines of code and containing custom kernels in different languages and vendor-dependent libraries. The interfaces provided by oneMKL enabled the seamless integration of SYCL RNGs into FastCaloSim with no code modification across the evaluated platforms. The SYCL 2020 interoperability functionality enabled custom kernels and vendor-dependent library integration to be abstracted out from the application, improving the maintainability of the application and reducing the source lines of code. The application yields comparable performance with the native approach on different architectures. Whereas the ISO C++ version of FastCaloSim had two separate codebases for x86 architectures and NVIDIA GPUs, the work presented here has enabled event processing on a variety of major vendor hardware from a single SYCL entry point. Hence, the SYCL RNG based integration facilitates the code maintainability by reducing the FastCaloSim code size without introducing any significant performance overhead.

While we have demonstrated that SYCL interoperability leads to reusability of existing optimized vendor-dependent libraries and enables cross-platform portability, devices without vendor libraries cannot be supported. For example, no RNG kernels exist yet for ARM Mali devices. One possible solution would be to provide pure SYCL kernel implementations for common RNG engines. The kernel could then be compiled for any device for which a SYCL-supported compiler exists. Moreover, in scientific applications and workflows where reproducibility is essential, kernels written entirely in the SYCL programming model can offer improved reliability across architectures and platforms. Although the portability of such an RNG kernel would be guaranteed, performance remains challenging and likely would necessitate mechanisms such as tuning of kernels for different architectures

Finally, extending performance portability to include also productivity and reproducibility in an objective way would general scientific applications and workflows aiming for architecture and platform independence.

Acknowledgement. This work was completed while V.R.P. was at Lawrence Berkeley National Laboratory, and was funded in part by the DOE HEP Center for Computational Excellence at Lawrence Berkeley National Laboratory under B&R KA2401045.

Data Availability Statement

Summary of the Experiments Reported

We ran two benchmark applications on a variety of hardware:

1. Intel Core i7-1080H, Intel UIID Graphics 630 (Razer Blade Studio Edition 2020) 2. AMD Rome 7742, NVIDIA A100 (DGX node from NERSC) 3. MSI Radeon RX Vega 56 (Private Intel Xeon Gold 5220 node).

Both applications are freely available (Github link below) but inputs to FastCaloSim are proprietary data of the ATLAS Experiment that we unfortunately cannot shared publicly (special access may be granted upon request).

We used Intel LLVM sycl-nightly/20210330, nvcc 10.2 and hipSYCL 0.9.0 for the various targets. oneMKL is used for all RNG but the hipRAND backend is not publicly available due to DOE restrictions on software developed by employees. We are happy to make arrangements for this to be made available.

Artifact Availability

Software Artifact Availability: All author-created software artifacts are maintained in a public repository under an OSI-approved license.

Hardware Artifact Availability: All author-created hardware artifacts are maintained in a public repository under an OSI-approved license.

Data Artifact Availability: Some author-created data artifacts are NOT maintained in a public repository or are NOT available under an OSI-approved license.

Proprietary Artifacts: There are associated proprietary artifacts that are not created by the authors. Some author-created artifacts are proprietary.

List of URLs and/or DOIs where artifacts are available:

```
https://github.com/oneapi-src/oneMKL
https://github.com/vrpascuzzi/FastCaloSim-GPU/tree/benchmarking
https://github.com/vrpascuzzi/benchprof/tree/sc21
```

Baseline Experimental Setup, and Modifications Made for the Paper

Relevant hardware details: DGX A100, Intel Core i7-1080H, Intel UHD Graphics 630, MSI Radeon RX Vega 56, NVIDIA A100, Intel Xeon Gold 5220

Operating systems and versions: Ubuntu 20.04 with kernel 5.8.18, OpenSUSE 15.0 with kernel 4.12, CentOS7 with kernel 3.10

Compilers and versions: GNU 8.2, nvcc 10.2, hipSCYL 0.9.0, Clang 12.0.0

Libraries and versions: oneMKL v0.1.0, CUDA 10.2.89, hip 4.0

Key algorithms: Philo $\times$ 4 $\times$ 32 $\times$ 10, MRG32k3a

Input datasets and versions: ATLAS FastCaloSim single-electron and top-antitop quark n-tuple inputs

Paper Modifications: We added to the oneMKL open-source interfaces library random number generator (RNG) support for AMD (hipRAND) and NVIDIA (cuRAND) GPUS through SYCL interoperability. This provides a single entry point for executing on a wide range of available HPC systems scientific and other codes which utilize RNGs.

Output from scripts that gathers execution environment information

A number of systems were used for these studies. As these studies
↪ were performed several months ago, and due to access
↪ privileges and updates, the hardware and software
↪ specifications are no longer valid. For example, the DGX node
↪ was a NERSC Perlmutter early access machine offered to
↪ Pascuzzi, and is no longer online.

For the most accurate details, please see "Baseline experimental
↪ setup, and modifications made for the paper" section above.

Artifact Evaluation

Verification and validation studies: Each experiment was run hundreds of times over the course of several weeks to validate day-to-day and operational fluctuations of the systems used for benchmarking.

Accuracy and precision of timings: Each experiment was run hundreds of times over the course of several weeks to validate day-to-day and operational fluctuations of the systems used for benchmarking.

Used manufactured solutions or spectral properties: N/A

Quantified the sensitivity of results to initial conditions and/or parameters of the computational environment: Each experiment was run hundreds of times over the course of several weeks to validate day-to-day and operational fluctuations of the systems used for benchmarking.

References

1. AMD hipBLAS: Dense Linear Algebra on AMD GPUs. https://github.com/ROCmSoftwarePlatform/hipBLAS. Accessed 05 Apr 2021
2. AMD hipRAND: Random Number Generation on AMD GPUs. https://github.com/ROCmSoftwarePlatform/rocRAND. Accessed 05 Apr 2021
3. ComputeCpp: Codeplay's implementation of the SYCL open standard. https://developer.codeplay.com/products/computecpp/ce/home. Accessed 28 Feb 2021
4. hipSYCL   RPMs.   http://repo.urz.uni-heidelberg.de/sycl/test-plugin/rpm/centos7/. Accessed 13 Mar 2021
5. Intel Math Kernel Library. https://intel.ly/32eX1eu. Accessed 31 Aug 2020
6. Intel oneAPI DPC++/C++ Compiler. https://github.com/intel/llvm/tree/sycl. Accessed 28 Feb 2021
7. Intel oneAPI Math Kernel Library (oneMKL). https://docs.oneapi.com/versions/latest/onemkl/index.html. Accessed 28 Feb 2021
8. NVIDIA cuBLAS: Dense Linear Algebra on GPUs. https://developer.nvidia.com/cublas. Accessed 31 Aug 2020

9. NVIDIA CUDA programming model. http://www.nvidia.com/CUDA. Accessed 05 Apr 2021
10. NVIDIA cuRAND: Random Number Generation on NVIDIA GPUs. https://developer.nvidia.com/curand. Accessed 28 Feb 2021
11. NVIDIA cuSPARSE: the CUDA sparse matrix library. https://docs.nvidia.com/cuda/cusparse/index.html. Accessed 05 Apr 2021
12. SYCL: C++ Single-source Heterogeneous Programming for OpenCL. https://www.khronos.org/registry/SYCL/specs/sycl-2020-provisional.pdf. Accessed 23 July 2020
13. The ARM Computer Vision and Machine Learning library. https://github.com/ARM-software/ComputeLibrary/. Accessed 31 Aug 2020
14. Aad, G., et al.: The ATLAS Experiment at the CERN Large Hadron Collider, vol. 3, p. S08003, 437 (2008). https://doi.org/10.1088/1748-0221/3/08/S08003, https://cds.cern.ch/record/1129811, also published by CERN Geneva in 2010
15. Agostinelli, S., et al.: GEANT4-a simulation toolkit, vol. 506, pp. 250–303 (2003). https://doi.org/10.1016/S0168-9002(03)01368-8
16. Alpay, A., Heuveline, V.: SYCL beyond OpenCL: the architecture, current state and future direction of hipSYCL. In: Proceedings of the International Workshop on OpenCL, p. 1 (2020)
17. Buckley, A., et al.: General-purpose event generators for LHC physics. Phys. Rep. **504**(5), 145–233 (2011)
18. Costanzo, M., Rucci, E., Sanchez, C.G., Naiouf, M.: Early Experiences Migrating CUDA codes to oneAPI (2021)
19. Deakin, T., McIntosh-Smith, S.: Evaluating the performance of HPC-Style SYCL applications. In: Proceedings of the International Workshop on OpenCL, IWOCL 2020. Association for Computing Machinery, New York (2020). https://doi.org/10.1145/3388333.3388643
20. Dong, Z., Gray, H., Leggett, C., Lin, M., Pascuzzi, V.R., Yu, K.: Porting HEP parameterized calorimeter simulation code to GPUs. Front. Big Data **4**, 32 (2021)
21. Edwards, H.C., Trott, C.R., Sunderland, D.: Kokkos: enabling manycore performance portability through polymorphic memory access patterns. J. Parallel Distrib. Comput. **74**, 3202–3216 (2014)
22. Feickert, M., Nachman, B.: A Living Review of Machine Learning for Particle Physics (2021)
23. Goli, M., et al.: Towards cross-platform performance portability of DNN models using SYCL. In: 2020 IEEE/ACM International Workshop on Performance, Portability and Productivity in HPC (P3HPC), pp. 25–35. IEEE (2020)
24. Gozillon, A., Keryell, R., Yu, L.Y., Harnisch, G., Keir, P.: triSYCL for Xilinx FPGA. In: The 2020 International Conference on High Performance Computing and Simulation. IEEE (2020)
25. Hornung, R.D., Keasler, J.A.: The RAJA portability layer: overview and status. Lawrence Livermore National Laboratory (LLNL), Livermore, CA (United States) (2014)
26. James, F., Moneta, L.: Review of high-quality random number generators. Comput. Softw. Big Comput. **4**, 1–12 (2020). https://doi.org/10.1007/s41781-019-0034-3
27. Larkin, J.: Performance portability through descriptive parallelism. In: Presentation at DOE Centers of Excellence Performance Portability Meeting (2016)
28. McIntosh-Smith, S., Boulton, M., Curran, D., Price, J.: On the performance portability of structured grid codes on many-core computer architectures. In: Kunkel, J.M., Ludwig, T., Meuer, H.W. (eds.) ISC 2014. LNCS, vol. 8488, pp. 53–75. Springer, Cham (2014). https://doi.org/10.1007/978-3-319-07518-1_4

29. Pennycook, S.J., Sewall, J.D., Lee, V.W.: Implications of a metric for performance portability. Future Gener. Comput. Syst. **92**, 947–958 (2019)
30. Pheatt, C.: Intel threading building blocks. J. Comput. Sci. Coll. **23**(4), 298 (2008)
31. Schaarschmidt, J.: The new ATLAS fast calorimeter simulation. J. Phys. Conf. Ser. **898**, 042006 (2017). https://doi.org/10.1088/1742-6596/898/4/042006
32. Stauber, T., Sommerlad, P.: ReSYCLator: transforming CUDA C++ source code into SYCL. In: Proceedings of the International Workshop on OpenCL, IWOCL 2019. Association for Computing Machinery, New York (2019). https://doi.org/10.1145/3318170.3318190
33. Stone, J.E., Gohara, D., Shi, G.: OpenCL: a parallel programming standard for heterogeneous computing systems. Comput. Sci. Eng. **12**(3), 66 (2010)
34. Zhu, W., Niu, Y., Gao, G.R.: Performance portability on EARTH: a case study across several parallel architectures. Cluster Comput. **10**(2), 115–126 (2007)

Directive Extensions

Extending OpenMP for Machine Learning-Driven Adaptation

Chunhua Liao[1(✉)], Anjia Wang[2], Giorgis Georgakoudis[1],
Bronis R. de Supinski[1], Yonghong Yan[2], David Beckingsale[1],
and Todd Gamblin[1]

[1] Lawrence Livermore National
Laboratory, Livermore, CA 94550, USA
{liao6,georgakoudis1,bronis,
beckingsale1,gamblin2}@llnl.gov
[2] University of North Carolina
at Charlotte, Charlotte, NC 28223, USA
{awang15,yyan7}@uncc.edu

Abstract. OpenMP 5.0 introduced the `metadirective` directive to support compile-time selection from a set of directive variants based on OpenMP context. OpenMP 5.1 extended context information to include user-defined conditions that enable user-guided runtime adaptation. However, defining conditions that capture the complex interactions between applications and hardware platforms to select an optimized variant is challenging for programmers. This paper explores a novel approach to automate runtime adaptation through machine learning. We design a new `declare adaptation` directive to describe semantics for model-driven adaptation and also develop a prototype implementation. Using the Smith-Waterman algorithm as a use-case, our experiments demonstrate that the proposed adaptive OpenMP extension automatically chooses the code variants that deliver the best performance in heterogeneous platforms that consist of CPU and GPU processing capabilities. Using decision tree models for tuning has an accuracy of up to 93.1% in selecting the optimal variant, with negligible runtime overhead.

Keywords: OpenMP · Machine Learning · Runtime Adaptation

1 Introduction

Variant directives such as metadirective and declare variant are major new features introduced in OpenMP 5.0 [18] to improve performance portability by adapting OpenMP pragmas and user code at compile time. The OpenMP context, which consists of traits from active OpenMP constructs, devices, implementations or user-defined conditions, can guide adaptation. For example, the metadirective is conditionally resolved at compile time based on traits that define an OpenMP condition or context to select one of multiple directive variants. Based on a recommendation from a prior study [27], OpenMP 5.1 [19] added a new dynamic

S. Bhalachandra et al. (Eds.): WACCPD 2021, LNCS 13194, pp. 49–69, 2022.
https://doi.org/10.1007/978-3-030-97759-7_3

trait set that supports user-defined conditions. As a result, OpenMP programmers can now use dynamic conditions to guide the selection of directive variants. A canonical example is a user-defined loop iteration threshold (in a form of N >=50000) to decide if a parallel loop should execute on CPUs or GPUs.

While the `metadirective` enables runtime code adaptation, it falls to the programmer to determine the conditions upon which to select the best performing code variant. However, manually determining the appropriate conditions (such as the loop iteration threshold) is challenging. Meaningful values depend on complex interactions between applications and hardware platforms, thus by definition programmer choices are not portable. Further, there are many options and configurations of OpenMP compilation and the supporting runtime software that contribute to complexity, given the software stack configuration affects performance. Thus, users would benefit from automated mechanisms to select the best performing variant without manually specifying non-portable and error-prone runtime conditions.

In this paper, we explore a novel, portable approach of incorporating machine learning capabilities into OpenMP to automatically derive models used as dynamic conditions that guide directive variant selection. This paper makes the following contributions:

- A new directive and associated clauses to express essential semantics to achieve automated model-driven runtime adaptation of a given OpenMP region;
- Compiler transformations that enable runtime profiling, model building, and model-guided adaptation of an adaptive OpenMP region; and
- Extensions to a tuning runtime library that provides a small but powerful set of novel APIs to support the multiple stages needed for model-driven adaptation.

Experimentation shows that our adaptive OpenMP extension is able to select the best performing variant for the Smith-Waterman algorithm, which is particularly hard to tune, for a range of input sizes, on heterogeneous platforms with CPU and GPU processing capabilities.

2   A Motivating Example

We use the Smith-Waterman algorithm [22] to demonstrate the need for automated OpenMP adaptation. This dynamic algorithm finds the optimal local alignment of a subsequence within a larger DNA or RNA sequence by calculating a distance (or similarity) matrix. The scoring process has a wavefront computation pattern, as Fig. 1 shows, due to data dependencies between points of the matrix computation. The algorithm has $O(M \times N)$ time complexity in which M and N are the lengths of the two sequences. The space complexity is also $O(M \times N)$ due to matrices used for computing scores and backtracking.

Figure 2 shows a typical OpenMP CPU implementation of the Smith-Waterman algorithm's scoring step. It parallelizes the inner loop iterating on elements of each wavefront line. Similarly, Fig. 3 shows an OpenMP GPU offload version, which moves the data used on GPU before the outer loop, and copies back results after processing completes to reduce data transfer overheads.

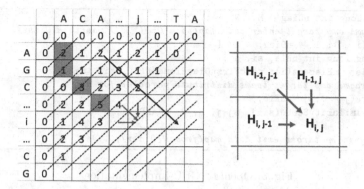

Fig. 1. Wavefront Computation Pattern of the Smith-Waterman Algorithm

```
1  long long int nDiag = M + N - 1;
2  for (i = 1; i <= nDiag; ++i) {
3    long long int nEle, si, sj;
4    nEle = nElement(i); calcFirstDiagElement(i, &si, &sj);
5    #pragma omp parallel for
6    for (j = 0; j < nEle; ++j)
7      similarityScore(si-j, sj+j, H, P, &maxPos);
8  }
```

Fig. 2. OpenMP CPU Implementation of the Smith-Waterman Algorithm

We compare the performance of three versions (serial CPU, OpenMP CPU and OpenMP GPU) for two sequences of equal input lengths, by ranging their length from 32 to 15,000 with a stride of 256. Our comparison uses one compute node of the Corona cluster of the Livermore Computing Center. It has two AMD EPYC 7401 processors, each with 24 cores clocked at 2 GHz, 250 GB memory, and four AMD MI50 GPUs. We compile with Clang 12.0.0 and ROCm v4.1.0, with the −O3 option. Figure 4 shows the scoring kernel execution time. The serial version performs the best for input sizes ranging from 32 to 6048. From 6304 to 8864, the OpenMP GPU version is the best choice. Finally, the OpenMP CPU version performs the best for input problem sizes ranging from 9120 to 15,000. It would be challenging for programmers to manually determine such conditions to select the best variants for different software and hardware configurations.

In general, the optimal choice among OpenMP variants varies significantly depending on the application kernels, input sizes, machines and compilers. Manual specifying conditions guiding the optimal choice is neither practical nor portable. Thus, we propose a new mechanism to automate adaptation without user intervention.

```
1   long long int nDiag = M + N - 1;
2   #pragma omp target enter data map(to:a[0:m],...) map(to:H[0:asz],...)
3   for (i = 1; i <= nDiag; ++i) {
4     long long int nEle, si, sj;
5     nEle = nElement(i); calcFirstDiagElement(i, &si, &sj);
6     #pragma omp target teams distribute parallel for map (...)
7     for (j = 0; j < nEle; ++j)
8       similarityScore(si-j, sj+j, H, P, &maxPos);
9   }
10  #pragma omp target exit data map(from:H[0:asz],...)
```

Fig. 3. OpenMP GPU Implementation

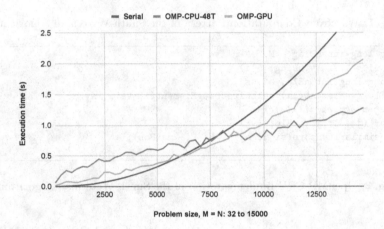

Fig. 4. Performance of Three Versions of Smith-Waterman Running on Corona

3   A Vision

We envision that future programming models, including OpenMP, will allow programmers to express rich semantics related to automated adaptation using machine learning techniques. Seamless integration of programming models and machine learning has multiple benefits. For one, direct support in a programming model will make machine learning techniques more accessible. Programmers will be relieved from manually assembling machine learning pipelines to optimize each program. Further, the integration will improve performance portability and productivity of programming systems.

As Fig. 5 shows, we extend OpenMP to enable machine learning-driven adaptation. Our extension uses a new directive, **declare adaptation**, to generate transformed (or lowered) code variants for each annotated code region. The lowered code implements an execution pipeline that includes profiling, model building and adaptation. Common functionality in those steps is supported by a runtime library to simplify the compiler transformation.

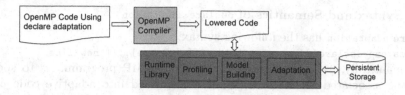

Fig. 5. Machine Learning-Driven Adaptive OpenMP

A generated executable file may run in different modes. The first run transparently collects profiling data for selected adaptive code regions. Once sufficient data is collected, the executable automatically builds a predictive machine learning model for each selected code region. Finally, the internally generated machine learning models guide runtime selection of the best variants for each region. Profiling, model building and model-driven adaptation may finish within the first run of a program, especially for those that use iterative algorithms, which often can easily generate sufficient training data.

The extended OpenMP also supports collecting profiling data across multiple runs, which is essential if a single run does not generate sufficient training data. Those profiling data accumulate in persistent storage to enable model building and adaptation in later runs. Also, previously trained models are saved too for reuse in later runs, avoiding unnecessary profiling and model building. In summary, the execution of an adaptive OpenMP program checks if previous profiling data or machine learning models are available in order to initialize adaptive execution. The following sections elaborate on the design and implementation of the declare adaptation directive.

4   The declare adaptation Directive

The proposed declare adaptation allows programmers to express semantics related to machine learning-driven automatic runtime adaptation. In our present design, declare adaptation works with metadirectives. Code regions annotated with metadirecive naturally provide multiple directive variants for adaptation. Future work will explore its composability with other directives.

When a code region enclosed by metadirective immediately follows the declare adaptation directive, each when and default clause is treated as a code variant that can be automatically selected. Internally, each code variant is assigned a unique variant ID, starting from 0.

Using declare adaptation overrides the context-selector-specifications of the when clauses, using instead user-provided features as part of the adaptation directive to model the performance of possible variants and select the predicted optimal one. Programmers can also entirely avoid specifying context selectors in the metadirective. The machine must support a valid execution context to enable the execution of all variants of the metadirective so the runtime can freely activate any of them for profiling, modeling and subsequent selection.

4.1   Syntax and Semantics of `declare adaptation`

`declare adaptation` has the following syntax:

`#pragma omp declare adaptation [clause[[,]clause]...] new-line`.

Semantically, `declare adaptation` allows OpenMP programmers to specify that the associated OpenMP region is transformed into adaptive code using online performance profiling and model-driven adaptation. The compiler generates a lowered multi-variant code region, leveraging runtime functions to support profiling, model building and tuning, as Fig. 5 shows.

The possible associated clauses are the following:

- `model(model_type_name)`,
- `feature([modifiers]: list)`,
- `model_name(region_id)`,
- `use_model(region_id)`, and
- `variant_mapping(list-of-mapped-model-region-variant-ids)`.

The parameter of the optional `model` clause indicates the type of machine learning model to use. If this clause is not specified, the model type is implementation defined. Values of `model_type_name` are supervised machine learning models for classification problems, such as `logistic_regression`, `decision_tree`, `random_forest`, `artificial_neural_network` and `support_vector_machine`.

The mandatory `feature` clause specifies a list of variables that serve as model features. Any program variable in scope may be used as a feature of the machine learning model. In addition, we assume that a set of special OpenMP variable identifiers, including `omp_num_threads` and `omp_num_teams`, are available to enable modeling of the OpenMP context. The clause may be repeated as often as necessary to describe all variables that the model should use as features.

Further, the `feature` clause accepts two optional modifiers that specify additional information for listed items. An example is `feature (range[0:30000]`, `min_sample_points(25): N)`. The `[lower_bound:upper_bound]` argument of the `range` modifier specifies a range expression for the variables in `list`. Both bounds are inclusive values of either integer or floating point types that define a search space of feature values. The integer argument of the `min_sample_points` modifier is a hint on the number of data points to sample for those features. This modifier guides the implementation in determining if sufficient data have been gathered for adaptation. A possible formula for an implementation is $Min\_dataset\_size = (min\_f1 \times min\_f2 \times \cdots \times min\_fn) \times code\_variant\_count$. For example, a code region with 3 code variants and 2 feature variables of `min_sample_points(10)` has a suggested training set size of $10 * 10 * 3 = 300$ data points.

The `model_name` and `use_model` clauses specify the model for guiding this region's adaptation and they form an exclusive clause set. This means that at most one of them can be used within a `declare adaptation` directive. If neither clause is specified, the effect is as if `model_name` is specified with an implementation-defined unique `region_id`. The `model_name` clause indicates that the associated region is a primary region for profiling, model building, and model-driven adaptation. An example primary region is a loop doing intensive computation. The user must specify a unique identifier for the region in the `model_id` argument. The `use_model` clause indicates that this region is an associated region to a primary region, so it should use the choices made by that corresponding primary region's model. An example associated region is a data transferring region preparing data for later computation. Its required argument specifies the ID of its primary region. Multiple regions may use the primary region's model.

The `variant_mapping` clause is valid and required only if the `use_model` clause is specified. It establishes a code variant mapping between a primary region and the associated region. The required mapping allows the region to have a different number of variants from the primary region. It specifies which variant an implementation should use based on the model decision of the primary region. The size of the list of mappings is equal to the number of code variants of the associated region. Each list item is a code variant ID of the corresponding primary region. For example, `variant_mapping(2,3)` means that the associated region has 2 code variants (with IDs 0 and 1) that are mapped to variant IDs 2 and 3 of the corresponding primary region. The associated region must not have more code variants than the region specified by `region_id`.

4.2 Examples Using `metadirective`

We demonstrate the use of `declare adaptation` within the Smith-Waterman algorithm. Figure 6 shows two nested loops that comprise the similarity score computation kernel. Our version specifies three code variants using a `metadirective`: serial, OpenMP CPU threading, and OpenMP GPU offloading (line 7–11). We use `declare adaptation` on line 6, right before `metadirective`, to specify a decision tree model trained on a single feature (`nDiag` derived from the lengths of the two sequences), which is the number of the wavefront lines of the similarity matrix. For two sequences with size M and N, the following relationship holds: $nDiag - M + N - 1$.

The choice of `nDiag` instead of the inner loop bound `nEle` is based on experiments of a prior study [27] which reports that `nDiag` is a good indicator for tuning. Choosing `nDiag` means that for a given pair of M and N values, a single code variant is activated for the entire execution of the program. So adaptation happens at a coarse granularity across different executions of the entire program. In comparison, if we choose `nEle`, adaptation happens at a fine granularity, across different wavefront lines. This fine-grain adaptation requires data transfers inside the outer loop, which introduces excessive data copy overhead across wavefront lines as Fig. 6 shows. Our experiments on Corona confirms that this overhead results in severe performance degradation compared to its baseline serial version using input sizes of 2000 by 2000 (56 s for the fine-grain adaptation version vs. 0.04 s for the serial version), hence the motivation for coarse grain adaptation.

A further optimization is using a data region that encloses both the outer and inner loop. Thus, data is copied between devices only when entering and exiting that region. We render the data region's execution adaptive by adding two more adaptive `metadirective` definitions (line 2–5 and 25–27 in Fig. 7). Variant selection for those two regions corresponds to the decision made for the primary region (line 13–21). When the primary region's variant ID 2 is active at runtime,

```
1    for (i = 1; i <= nDiag; ++i) {
2      long long int nEle, si, sj;
3      nEle = nElement(i);
4      calcFirstDiagElement(i, &si, &sj);
5
6    #pragma omp declare adaptation model(decision_tree) feature(nDiag)
7    #pragma omp metadirective \
8      when (:)                    /* variant 0: serial*/ \
9      when (:parallel for)        /* variant 1: CPU threading */ \
10     default(target teams distribute parallel for map (to:a[0:m], ...) \
11           map(tofrom: H[0:asz], ...) /* variant 2: GPU offloading */
12     for (j = 0; j < nEle; ++j)
13       similarityScore(si-j, sj+j, H, P, &maxPos);
14   }
```

Fig. 6. Basic Use of `declare adaptation` with `metadirective`

which selects GPU execution, the two associated regions are activated (using `variant_mapping(2)`). This example also shows that when an associated region executes before its primary region, the corresponding feature variables should be available at the entry point of this associated region for model evaluation. Also, the values of those variables should not change before entering the primary region, thus stay invariant. Then it is possible for the runtime to activate the mapped variants in both regions. Otherwise, a primary region should execute before its associated regions to forward its model decision.

5   Implementation

We design and implement a compiler-runtime system that translates OpenMP programs with the `declare adaptation` directive into adaptive executables. Figure 8 shows that our source-to-source compiler (based on ROSE [21]) translates an OpenMP program that uses `declare adaptation` into lowered adaptive OpenMP code. We then translate that representation into a final executable using Clang/LLVM. The lowered adaptive OpenMP code and our runtime system (based on Apollo [4,26]) implement runtime profiling, model building and model-guided adaptation. The runtime uses the OpenCV machine learning library [7] to build machine learning models from profiling data. To support reuse of profiling data and ML models across executions, the runtime system loads and stores training data and models between main memory and persistent storage (e.g., the file system).

5.1   Compiler Support

We use ROSE to prototype our compiler implementation. Developed at LLNL, ROSE [21] is an open source compiler infrastructure to build source-to-source program transformation and analysis tools for Fortran and C/C++ applications.

```
1   //Copy the data to GPU if the GPU version will be used later.
2   //Primary region's variant #2 is mapped to variant id #0 here.
3   #pragma omp declare adaptation use_model("scoring_loop") variant_mapping(2)
4   #pragma omp metadirective \
5    when(: target enter data map(to:a[0:m],...) map(to:H[0:asz],...))
6
7   for (i = 1; i <= nDiag; ++i) {
8     long long int nEle, si, sj;
9     nEle = nElement(i);
10    calcFirstDiagElement(i, &si, &sj);
11
12  // The primary region with 3 variants
13  #pragma omp declare adaptation model_name("scoring_loop") \
14     model(decision_tree) feature(nDiag)
15     #pragma omp metadirective \
16     when (: ) \
17     when (: parallel for private(j)) \
18     default (target teams distribute parallel for ...)
19     for (j = 0; j < nEle; ++j)
20       similarityScore(si-j, sj+j, H, P, &maxPos);
21  }
22
23  //Copy data back to CPU if GPU is used
24  //Primary region's variant #2 is mapped to variant id #0 here.
25  #pragma omp declare adaptation use_model("scoring_loop") variant_mapping(2)
26  #pragma omp metadirective \
27   when( : target exit data map(from: H[0:asz], P[0:asz], maxPos))
```

Fig. 7. Optimized Use of `declare adaption`

ROSE supports OpenMP 3.0 [13] and part of 4.0 [15]. More recently, it was used to prototype the dynamic extension of metadirective [27].

Our prototype compiler includes an extended OpenMP parser and internal AST to support `declare adaptation`. It also translates an AST that represents a `metadirective` region affected by `declare adaptation` into one that uses a switch-case statement to enable machine-learning based adaptation. We lower that AST into source files that use OpenMP 4.5 directives (using CPU threading and GPU offloading directives). Finally, Clang/LLVM compiles the lowered code and links it with the Apollo runtime library to generate the final executable.

The lowered code uses several runtime interface functions to support all stages in the model-driven adaptation workflow. The workflow first collects execution time of variants associated with user-specified features of a code region. It then processes those data into feature vectors suitable for machine learning and feeds those training data into OpenCV to generate the model. Finally, it evaluates at runtime the generated model to select code variants.

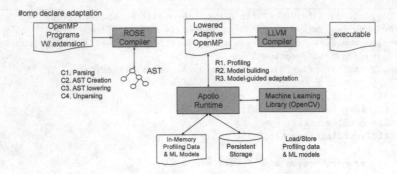

Fig. 8. Design and Implementation of Adaptive OpenMP

Figure 9 shows the lowered code for the input code in Fig. 7. Each code variant of a `metadirective` region under `declare adaptation` control is placed in a `case` statement of a `switch` statement. We synchronize the primary and the associated adaptive regions using a region name identifier and variant ID numbers. In this example, the two corresponding regions that copy data between the CPU and GPU are only activated when the primary region's code variant 2 (GPU offloading version) is activated. The lowering step leverages runtime support to reuse the same generated code for different stages of the workflow. For example, we use the `getPolicyIndex()` function at line 27 to pick a policy to support both training and production runs. Details of the runtime support are explained in the next subsection.

5.2   Runtime Support

We extend Apollo [4, 26] to serve as our runtime library. Apollo was originally applied as an auto-tuning extension of RAJA [12] that uses pre-trained, reusable machine learning models to tune data-dependent kernels at runtime. Nevertheless, Apollo's modular design simplifies support of runtime adaptation for non-RAJA codes, OpenMP in our case.

For adaptive code regions, an internal C++ Region class tracks the associated features, manages training data and activates the model. Each code region can have multiple code variants, such as one for CPU and another for GPU. Apollo treats each variant as a distinct execution policy of the region to measure its execution time. The runtime uses these measured times to train a machine learning model for suggesting the best execution policy, which corresponds to the fastest code variant.

Apollo exposes a small set of runtime API functions to support data collection, model building and model-guided adaptation through two concepts: training models and tuning models. Training models are special models that activate different code variants to collect data during training runs, while tuning models are generated machine learning models to select optimal code variants (or equivalently execution policies) to activate during production runs. The active model

```
1   /* 1. Translation of the first dependent region*/
2   /* Create or obtain the main region*/
3   /* Parameters: unique region id, feature count, and variant count. */
4   Apollo::Region *region1 =
5   Apollo::instance()->getRegion("scoring-loop", 1,  3);
6   /* feature vector of size 1 */
7   region1->begin({(float)nDiag} );
8
9   // Get the policy to execute from Apollo
10  int policy = region1->getPolicyIndex();
11  if (policy ==2)
12  {
13    #pragma omp target enter data map(to:a[0:m-1], b[0:n-1]) \
14      map(to: H[0:asz], P[0:asz], maxPos)
15  }
16  region1->end();
17
18  for (i = 1; i <= nDiag; ++i) {
19    /* ....some code omitted here... */
20
21    /* 2. Translation of main adaptation  region*/
22    Apollo::Region *region = Apollo::instance()->getRegion(
23    "scoring-loop", 1, 3, 1);
24    region->begin({ (float)nDiag });
25
26    /* calling a training or real model to select a code variant */
27    int policy = region->getPolicyIndex();
28
29    switch (policy)   {
30      case 0:  /* variant 0: serial */
31      { /*  code omitted here  */}
32      case 1: /* variant 1: CPU threading */
33      {
34      #pragma omp parallel for
35      for (j = 0; j < nEle; ++j)
36        similarityScore(si-j, sj+j, H, P, &maxPos);
37      break;
38      }
39      case 2: /* variant 2: GPU offloading */
40      {
41      #pragma omp target teams distribute parallel for map (...)
42      for (j = 0; j < nEle; ++j)
43        similarityScore(si-j, sj+j, H, P, &maxPos);
44      break;
45      }
46      default:
47        /* .. error handling here... */
48    }
49    region->end();
50  }
51
52  /* 3. Translation of the 2nd dependent region, code omitted here*/
```

Fig. 9. Lowered Code Enabling Profiling, Model Building and Adaptation

field of the Region class can be set to a training or tuning model. Thus, Apollo re-uses the same API interface function, `getPolicyIndex()` to return either a training or optimal code variant, which simplifies the compiler transformation.

Apollo provides two builtin training models (Random and Round-Robin) to support profiling code variants. A training run with a given input data may invoke a region multiple times and at every invocation the Random model randomly selects a code variant of the region to measure performance. Similarly, the Round-Robin model cyclically selects each code variant for performance profiling. By default, Apollo averages the measured execution times for each code variant when collecting measurements during training. The tuning models include the Static model (returns a fixed policy choice) and a set of machine learning models supported by OpenCV such as Decision Tree, Random Forest and Support Vector Machine.

We extend Apollo in several ways. Specifically, we add support for collecting and accumulating profiling data across multiple executions to ensure there is sufficient training data for model building. Original Apollo requires an explicit function call to trigger model building. We automatically trigger model building when sufficient data have been collected based on the semantics of `declare adaptation`. Additionally, we apply the Static model as a training model to support coarse grain adaptation, by using a fixed code variant throughout an entire program execution for a given input data size. Lastly, we add a new configuration option to use the accumulated total execution time instead of the average time as the input performance feature for OpenCV-generated models to enable coarse grain adaptation.

Overall, our implementation uses six runtime functions to support adaptation. `Apollo* Apollo::instance()` is used to initialize the runtime and obtain a handle to it.

`Apollo::Region* Apollo::getRegion (string& region, int feature_count, int policy_count, int model_type)` obtains a managed code region's internal C++ object by its name. If the region object exists, the function directly returns it. Otherwise, the runtime creates and initializes it, using the specified feature count, policy count, and machine learning model type. Each code region object's active model field is initialized to a tuning or training model. At first, the function tries to load an existing tuning model file saved on disk for the region. If the model file does not exist, a default training model (Static, Random or Round-Robin) is configured for the region. Similarly, if training across multiple executions is requested, the runtime tries to initialize the region object's training data field by loading an existing training dataset for the region from disk.

The `Apollo::Region::begin(std::vector<float>)` indicates the beginning of a managed code region. The parameter of this function is a vector of features of float type. The length of the vector matches the number of features of the code region. This function starts a timer for the managed code region.

`Apollo::Region::getPolicyIndex()` calls the active model associated with the code region to return a preferred policy ID. If the model is a training model, it picks a variant for profiling. Otherwise, a tuning model (such as a decision tree model) selects an optimal code variant by evaluating the model with the set features associated with the region as inputs.

`Apollo::Region::end()` stops the timer for the managed code region and adds information (such as the measured execution time, the executed policy, and the feature vector) into the region's training data field. Additionally, if the average execution time is used as training data, it checks if sufficient profiling data have been collected for the region, in which case the function triggers data processing and model building using the collected data. Also, it stores the generated model for later use.

`Apollo::~Apollo()`, the destructor of the Apollo runtime object, is implicitly called when a program ends. If the accumulated total execution time of regions is used to train models, this function will check if sufficient training data have been collected and trigger model building for later re-use. It saves any collected training data and generated models to disk.

6 Evaluation

6.1 Software and Hardware Configurations

We evaluate the effectiveness of the proposed OpenMP extension using the adaptive Smith-Waterman algorithm shown in Fig. 7. The corresponding serial, OpenMP CPU threading, and OpenMP GPU offloading versions are used as baseline, non-adaptive versions. Picking `nDiag` as the feature requires multiple runs using different problem sizes to collect training data. The minimal sample points per feature (specified using `min_sample_points(val)`) is configured to have three values: 25, 50, or 100. During the training runs, the input problem size range is fixed to be between 32 to 15,000. Three different strides (128, 256 and 512) in that range are used to generate sufficient training data for the three sampling configurations.

For each input problem size, all code variants are measured in the same batched run for collecting training data. The training run is repeated five times and median values are used as performance measurements. Decision tree models are created and stored in `yaml` files for later reuse. Once the model files are available, the execution of the program enters the production run mode. Different input problem sizes (160 to 15,000 with a stride of 256) are picked to evaluate the generated models in production runs.

Two machines, Corona and Pascal, are used for the experiments, with their details shown in Table 1. For the OpenMP CPU version, we use the number of threads matching the number of physical cores on a machine to avoid system noise caused by oversubscribing CPU cores.

6.2 Performance Results

Figure 10 and 11 show the execution time of different versions of the Smith-Waterman algorithm on the two machines. The adaptive version uses the decision

Table 1. Software and Hardware Configurations

	LLNL Corona	LLNL Pascal
CPU	AMD EPYC 7401 2.00 GHz	Intel Xeon E5-2695 v4 2.10 GHz
Cores	2 sockets × 24 physical cores	2 sockets × 18 physical cores
Main Mem	256 GB	256 GB
GPU	AMD Radeon Instinct MI50	NVIDIA Tesla P100
Device Mem	16 GB	16 GB
OS	TOSS 3	Red Hat Enterprise Linux 7.6
Clang/LLVM	12.0.0	11.0.0
Compiler Options	−O3	−O3
GPU Driver	AMD ROCm 4.1.0	NVIDIA CUDA toolkit 10.2.89

tree model generated using the minimum sample points per feature set to 50. It is clear that the performance of the adaptive version, denoted with a green line, closely matches the best choices, especially for Pascal. On Corona, the adaptive version does not pick the serial version, which is the fastest, for input size range between 32 and 5,000. However, the execution time of the predicted variant is very close to serial, so performance is near-optimal anyway.

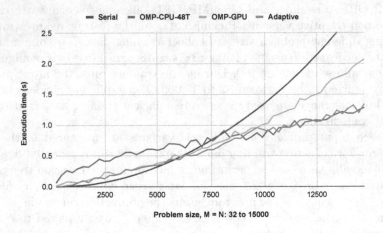

Fig. 10. Execution Time of Different Versions of Smith-Waterman on Corona

6.3   Accuracy of Prediction Models

The accuracy of the generated models is evaluated by comparing the predicted best code variants against the ground truth of optimal variants for a set of production runs using the selected input problem sizes. Note that we purposely select a different set of 58 input problem sizes (160 to 15,000 with a stride of 256) in the production run, which are unseen in the training runs. To generate

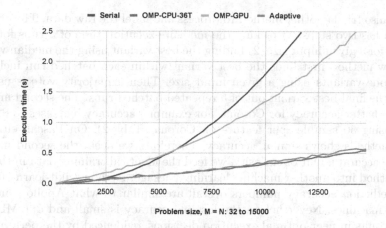

Fig. 11. Execution Time of Different Versions of Smith-Waterman on Pascal

the ground truth, we run the baseline versions using the same input problem sizes selected for the production runs to identify the fastest execution variant.

Table 2 shows the accuracy evaluation results. For the three values of minimal sample points per feature (25, 50 and 100), the created decision tree models show the best accuracy of 79.31% for Corona and 93.10% for Pascal (among table's columns named Median).

Table 2. Prediction Accuracy of Smith-Waterman under Multiple Configurations

Training samples	25			50			100		
Platform	Median	Majority Vote	Majority Vote (sklearn)	Median	Majority Vote	Majority Vote (sklearn)	Median	Majority Vote	Majority Vote (sklearn)
Corona	72.41%	77.59%	72.41%	79.31%	82.76%	84.48%	75.86%	77.59%	75.00%
Pascal	93.10%	93.10%	94.83%	93.10%	93.10%	93.10%	93.10%	93.10%	93.10%

We investigated possible causes for the limited accuracy of the models generated on Corona. It is observed that the serial version's timing information collected in the training data is not exactly the same as the corresponding baseline version without code instrumentation. The OpenMP CPU and GPU versions do not show such a problem. We suspect that code instrumentation (using runtime API calls) prevents the compiler from applying some optimizations on the serial version of the code. Both OpenMP versions already use outlining which hurts optimizations, so additional instrumentation causes much less negative impact. To test this hypothesis, we re-run the experiments with compiler optimizations turned off (using the −O0 compilation flag). The adaptive version then made 55 correct choices out of 58 input problem sizes, which leads to an accuracy of 94.83%. Only three sizes have wrong predictions. These three wrong predictions happen near the crossover points in Fig. 10 where different policies have similar performance.

We also tried another method to process and label the raw data. The original method has two steps: 1) picking the median execution time of 5 runs for each variant for a given input size, 2) finding the best variant using the median values. The new method first finds the best variant within each batched run including three code variants using a given input size. Then a majority vote is used to decide the final best variant out of 5 repeated batched runs. The second method leads to better accuracy for Corona. For example, accuracy increases to 82.76% when using 50 samples per feature on Corona (Table 2). On Pascal, either of those methods shows similar accuracy. Therefore, we deem the second method as more accurate. Out of curiosity, we feed the identical training data in the second method into another machine learning package, Python scikit-learn v0.24.2. The prediction accuracy numbers overall are similar to what Apollo generates on two machines. Nevertheless, the loss in accuracy is small and our ML approach results in near-optimal execution decisions, evidenced by the performance measurements.

6.4   Overhead Analysis

There are three kinds of overheads in the adaptive version: the one-off overhead to perform the training run for data collection, the one-off overhead for model building, and the instrumentation and model evaluation overhead in production runs. The observed overheads depend on many factors, including the number of data points, the input size of a program, and the choice of the machine learning model, To measure those overheads, we pick the configuration of using 50 sample points and three input problem sizes from 32 to 15,000, which are 4,128, 8,480, and 12,576.

Table 3. Execution Time of Baseline, Training and Production Runs on Corona

	Baseline Run			Training Run			Production Run	
M == N	Serial	OMP-CPU	OMP-GPU	Serial	OMP-CPU	OMP-GPU	Execution Time	Predicted Variant
4128	0.214	0.552	0.286	0.309	0.573	0.289	0.304	OMP-GPU
8480	0.967	0.871	0.803	1.094	0.798	0.793	0.757	OMP-GPU
12576	2.164	1.042	1.585	2.562	1.051	1.644	1.077	OMP-CPU

Table 3 shows the measured execution time for different runs using different configurations on Corona. Results on Pascal are similar, so we omit them. Table 4 shows overhead in percentage numbers for training runs and production runs. The serial variant's training runs have significantly high overhead compared to the corresponding baseline runs. For example, it took 0.309 s while its baseline version took only 0.214 s for the input size of 4,128, indicating an overhead of 44.74%. Again, the reason is that code instrumentation prevents certain compiler optimizations being applied, which has a more negative performance impact on the serial version than the OpenMP versions. We measured the training overhead of the serial version using −O0 compilation. The overhead then reduces significantly to 9.85% for the input size of 4,128.

The time cost of building the models is negligible. It took only 0.00684 s on average. The corresponding 95% confidence interval is 0.00684 ± 0.0038 s. It only happens once for a configuration. The code instrumentation and runtime adaptation in the production runs have overhead up to 6.28%.

Table 4. Overhead Percentage

M==N	Training Run			Production Run
	Serial	OMP-CPU	OMP-GPU	Predicted Variant
4128	44.74%	3.76%	1.05%	6.28%
8480	13.14%	−8.37%	−1.22%	−5.81%
12576	18.39%	0.84%	3.73%	3.28%

For the input size of 8480, there are three negative overhead numbers for the two training runs using OMP-CPU and OMP-GPU, and the production run. We looked into confidence interval values for the relevant measurements. The results show that the measured execution times of training and production runs do have significant overlapping with their baseline runs. For example, the baseline OMP-GPU has a confidence interval of 0.803 ± 0.0444 s while its production run's confidence interval is 0.757 ± 0.0553 s. As a result, we conclude that there is no statistically significant overhead.

Overall the implementation has negligible impact on execution time for training and production runs using CPUs or GPUs.

7 Related Work

Machine-learning based compiler optimization has been studied extensively for decades. Wang et al. [25] provide a comprehensive survey of machine learning techniques used to guide compiler optimization. Ashouri et al. [2] summarize machine learning techniques used to tackle two particular compiler optimization problems: optimization selection and phase-ordering. A notable project, Milepost GCC [9], combines production-quality GCC with machine learning to adapt to different architectures and predict profitable optimizations. Luk et al. [16] profile execution variants to build linear regression models in order to determine the optimal splitting ratio between CPU and GPU computation. Grewe et al. [10] uses decision tree models to decide if it is profitable to run OpenCL kernels on GPUs. Hayashi et al. [11] used offline, supervised machine-learning techniques to select preferred computing resources between CPUs and GPUs for individual Java kernels using a JIT compiler. DeepTune [8] uses raw code to develop a deep neural network to guide optimal mapping for OpenCL programs.

Given the flexibility of OpenMP, there is growing interest in autotuning of OpenMP programs to enable performance portability across different platforms. Liao et al. [14] apply source code outlining to enable autotuning of OpenMP loops from large applications. Sreenivasan et al. [23] introduce a lightweight OpenMP pragma autotuner to optimize scheduling policies, chunk sizes, and thread counts. In [20], the authors explored the benefits of using two OpenMP 5.0 features, including metadirective and declare variant, for the miniMD benchmark from the Mantevo suite. The authors concluded that these features enabled their code to be expressed in a more compact form while maintaining competitive performance portability across several architectures. However, their work only explored compile-time constant variables to express conditions.

Autotuning techniques are also well-studied for high performance computing, but dedicated mostly for loop transformation and for performance optimization, such as those in earlier works including POET [28] and CHILL [5]. Recent work, such as OpenTuner [1], provides a general-purpose optimization tool that could help users find the best configuration to improve the performance over a group of compilation parameters as search space. CLTune [17], as a generic tuner for OpenCL kernel, adopts a similar strategy. Active Harmony [24] is a runtime tuning framework for searching tuning variables for the configuration that delivers optimal performance. Indicatively, 3D-FFT has shown $1.76\times$ speedup when using online tuning methods implemented with Active Harmony. Another Active Harmony-based tool, named ANGEL [6], is developed to tune multiple functions for balancing the trade-off between computing time and power consumption. Bari et al. in [3] present ARCS framework for tuning OpenMP program targeting on optimizing power consumption.

Our work differs from the aforementioned studies in that we define combined language, compiler and runtime support methods to directly incorporate machine learning into a programming model, which enables automated model-driven runtime adaptation. Our approach significantly enhances portability and productivity of OpenMP.

8   Conclusion

In this paper, we have proposed a new OpenMP extension, declare adaptation, for programmers to express semantics related to machine learning-driven runtime adaptation. This directive is used with metadirective to guide the selection of an optimal choice of an OpenMP code region with multiple variants, using a machine learning model automatically built from user-specified features. Experimentation shows that this new extension improves the performance portability and productivity of OpenMP by alleviating the problem of manually deciding adaptation conditions for different software and hardware configurations. Additionally, this approach makes machine learning techniques more easily accessible to HPC developers.

In the future, we plan to expand the declare adaptation directive to apply to more types of OpenMP directives besides metadirective. Leveraging the prototype for the combined compiler and runtime support, we intend to migrate the implementation to a production quality compiler, such as Clang/LLVM, and also evaluate our approach on more applications and more diverse platforms.

Acknowledgment. This work was performed under the auspices of the U.S. Department of Energy by Lawrence Livermore National Laboratory under Contract DE-AC52-07NA27344 (LLNL-CONF-826432). The OpenMP language extension work was supported by the U.S. Dept. of Energy, Office of Science, Advanced Scientific Computing Research. The compiler and runtime work were supported by LLNL-LDRD 21-ERD-018.

Artifact Availability Statement

Summary of the Experiments Reported: We ran Smith Waterman algorithm on LLNL's Corona and Pascal supercomputer. The detailed software configurations are given in the experiment section of the paper.

Software Artifact Availability: All author-created software artifacts are maintained in a public repository under an OSI-approved license.

Hardware Artifact Availability: There are no author-created hardware artifacts.

Data Artifact Availability: All author-created data artifacts are maintained in a public repository under an OSI-approved license.

Proprietary Artifacts: None of the associated artifacts, author-created or otherwise, are proprietary.

List of URLs and/or DOIs where artifacts are available:

https://doi.org/10.5281/zenodo.5706501

References

1. Ansel, J., et al.: OpenTuner: an extensible framework for program autotuning. In: Proceedings of the 23rd International Conference on Parallel Architectures and Compilation, pp. 303–316 (2014)
2. Ashouri, A.H., Killian, W., Cavazos, J., Palermo, G., Silvano, C.: A survey on compiler autotuning using machine learning. ACM Comput. Surv. (CSUR) **51**(5), 1–42 (2018)
3. Bari, M.A.S., et al.: ARCS: adaptive runtime configuration selection for power-constrained OpenMP applications. In: 2016 IEEE International Conference on Cluster Computing (CLUSTER), pp. 461–470, September 2016. https://doi.org/10.1109/CLUSTER.2016.39
4. Beckingsale, D., Pearce, O., Laguna, I., Gamblin, T.: Apollo: reusable models for fast, dynamic tuning of input-dependent code. In: 2017 IEEE International Parallel and Distributed Processing Symposium (IPDPS), pp. 307–316. IEEE (2017)
5. Chen, C., Chame, J., Hall, M.: CHiLL: a framework for composing high-level loop transformations. Technical report, Citeseer (2008)

6. Chen, R.S., Hollingsworth, J.K.: ANGEL: a hierarchical approach to multi-objective online auto-tuning. In: Proceedings of the 5th International Workshop on Runtime and Operating Systems for Supercomputers, pp. 1–8 (2015)
7. Culjak, I., Abram, D., Pribanic, T., Dzapo, H., Cifrek, M.: A brief introduction to OpenCV. In: 2012 Proceedings of the 35th International Convention MIPRO, pp. 1725–1730. IEEE (2012)
8. Cummins, C., Petoumenos, P., Wang, Z., Leather, H.: End-to-end deep learning of optimization heuristics. In: 2017 26th International Conference on Parallel Architectures and Compilation Techniques (PACT), pp. 219–232. IEEE (2017)
9. Fursin, G., et al.: Milepost GCC: machine learning enabled self-tuning compiler. Int. J. Parallel Prog. **39**(3), 296–327 (2011)
10. Grewe, D., Wang, Z., O'Boyle, M.F.: Portable mapping of data parallel programs to OpenCL for heterogeneous systems. In: Proceedings of the 2013 IEEE/ACM International Symposium on Code Generation and Optimization (CGO), pp. 1–10. IEEE (2013)
11. Hayashi, A., Ishizaki, K., Koblents, G., Sarkar, V.: Machine-learning-based performance heuristics for runtime CPU/GPU selection. In: Proceedings of the Principles and Practices of Programming on the Java Platform, pp. 27–36 (2015)
12. Hornung, R.D., Keasler, J.A.: The RAJA portability layer: overview and status (2014)
13. Liao, C., Quinlan, D.J., Panas, T., de Supinski, B.R.: A ROSE-based OpenMP 3.0 research compiler supporting multiple runtime libraries. In: Sato, M., Hanawa, T., Müller, M.S., Chapman, B.M., de Supinski, B.R. (eds.) IWOMP 2010. LNCS, vol. 6132, pp. 15–28. Springer, Heidelberg (2010). https://doi.org/10.1007/978-3-642-13217-9_2
14. Liao, C., Quinlan, D.J., Vuduc, R., Panas, T.: Effective source-to-source outlining to support whole program empirical optimization. In: Gao, G.R., Pollock, L.L., Cavazos, J., Li, X. (eds.) LCPC 2009. LNCS, vol. 5898, pp. 308–322. Springer, Heidelberg (2010). https://doi.org/10.1007/978-3-642-13374-9_21
15. Liao, C., Yan, Y., de Supinski, B.R., Quinlan, D.J., Chapman, B.: Early experiences with the OpenMP accelerator model. In: Rendell, A.P., Chapman, B.M., Müller, M.S. (eds.) IWOMP 2013. LNCS, vol. 8122, pp. 84–98. Springer, Heidelberg (2013). https://doi.org/10.1007/978-3-642-40698-0_7
16. Luk, C.K., Hong, S., Kim, H.: Qilin: exploiting parallelism on heterogeneous multiprocessors with adaptive mapping. In: 2009 42nd Annual IEEE/ACM International Symposium on Microarchitecture (MICRO), pp. 45–55. IEEE (2009)
17. Nugteren, C., Codreanu, V.: CLTune: a generic auto-tuner for OpenCL kernels. In: 2015 IEEE 9th International Symposium on Embedded Multicore/Many-Core Systems-on-Chip, pp. 195–202. IEEE (2015)
18. OpenMP Architecture Review Board: OpenMP Application Programming Interface 5.0, November 2018. https://www.openmp.org/wp-content/uploads/OpenMP-API-Specification-5.0.pdf
19. OpenMP Architecture Review Board: OpenMP Application Programming Interface 5.1, November 2020. https://www.openmp.org/wp-content/uploads/OpenMP-API-Specification-5-1.pdf
20. Pennycook, S.J., Sewall, J.D., Hammond, J.R.: Evaluating the impact of proposed OpenMP 5.0 features on performance, portability and productivity. In: 2018 IEEE/ACM International Workshop on Performance, Portability and Productivity in HPC (P3HPC), pp. 37–46, November 2018. https://doi.org/10.1109/P3HPC.2018.00007

21. Quinlan, D., Liao, C.: The ROSE source-to-source compiler infrastructure. In: Cetus Users and Compiler Infrastructure Workshop, in Conjunction with PACT, vol. 2011, p. 1. Citeseer (2011)
22. Smith, T.F., Waterman, M.S., et al.: Identification of common molecular subsequences. J. Mol. Biol. **147**(1), 195–197 (1981)
23. Sreenivasan, V., Javali, R., Hall, M., Balaprakash, P., Scogland, T.R.W., de Supinski, B.R.: A framework for enabling OpenMP autotuning. In: Fan, X., de Supinski, B.R., Sinnen, O., Giacaman, N. (eds.) IWOMP 2019. LNCS, vol. 11718, pp. 50–60. Springer, Cham (2019). https://doi.org/10.1007/978-3-030-28596-8_4
24. Tapus, C., Chung, I.H., Hollingsworth, J.K.: Active harmony: towards automated performance tuning. In: Proceedings of the 2002 ACM/IEEE Conference on Supercomputing, SC 2002, pp. 1–11. IEEE Computer Society Press, Washington, DC (2002)
25. Wang, Z., O'Boyle, M.: Machine learning in compiler optimization. Proc. IEEE **106**(11), 1879–1901 (2018)
26. Wood, C., et al.: Artemis: automatic runtime tuning of parallel execution parameters using machine learning. In: Chamberlain, B.L., Varbanescu, A.-L., Ltaief, H., Luszczek, P. (eds.) ISC High Performance 2021. LNCS, vol. 12728, pp. 453–472. Springer, Cham (2021). https://doi.org/10.1007/978-3-030-78713-4_24
27. Yan, Y., Wang, A., Liao, C., Scogland, T.R.W., de Supinski, B.R.: Extending OpenMP Metadirective semantics for runtime adaptation. In: Fan, X., de Supinski, B.R., Sinnen, O., Giacaman, N. (eds.) IWOMP 2019. LNCS, vol. 11718, pp. 201–214. Springer, Cham (2019). https://doi.org/10.1007/978-3-030-28596-8_14
28. Yi, Q., Seymour, K., You, H., Vuduc, R., Quinlan, D.: POET: parameterized optimizations for empirical tuning. In: 2007 IEEE International Parallel and Distributed Processing Symposium, pp. 1–8. IEEE (2007)

Directive Case Studies

GPU Porting of Scalable Implicit Solver with Green's Function-Based Neural Networks by OpenACC

Kohei Fujita[1,2]([✉]), Yuma Kikuchi[1], Tsuyoshi Ichimura[1,2,3], Muneo Hori[4],
Lalith Maddegedara[1], and Naonori Ueda[3]

[1] Earthquake Research Institute and Department of Civil Engineering,
The University of Tokyo, Tokyo, Japan
{fujita,kikuchi-y,ichimura,lalith}@eri.u-tokyo.ac.jp
[2] Center for Computational Science, RIKEN, Kobe, Japan
[3] Center for Advanced Intelligence Project, RIKEN, Tokyo, Japan
naonori.ueda@riken.jp
[4] Research Institute for Value-Added-Information Generation, Japan Agency
for Marine-Earth Science and Technology, Yokohama, Japan
horimune@jamstec.go.jp

Abstract. With the development of diverse computer architectures and diverse HPC applications, it is desirable to make performance portable applications that run on multiple architectures with relatively low development cost. Directive based programming models such as OpenACC have been developed for such purpose, and have been used successfully to port many equation-based HPC applications. As an example of porting of a class of HPC applications comprising both data-analytics methods and equation-based methods, we port an implicit solver with a neural network (NN)-type preconditioner for solving large-scale partial differential equation (PDE)-based problems. The scalable preconditioner is based on the Green's functions reflecting properties of the target PDE, which improves the accuracy and efficiency of using NNs for solving PDE-based problems. By kernel algorithm design suitable for the computer architecture and use of OpenACC, we enabled high performance on recent GPUs with relatively low development cost. Here, 64.4% of FP64 peak was obtained on NVIDIA A100 GPU-equipped nodes of AI Bridging Cloud Infrastructure at National Institute of Advanced Industrial Science and Technology, leading to 2.54-fold speedup from a highly-tuned GPU implementation of a widely used PDE solver algorithm and 38.9-fold speedup from OpenMP-based CPU implementation running on the same system. Furthermore, 83.4% weak scalability was obtained from 8 to 256 A100 GPUs on the same system, enabling solving large scale problems of up to 25.7 billion degrees-of-freedom with high performance.

Keywords: Performance portability · OpenACC · GPU computation · Implicit solver · Neural network-based preconditioning

© Springer Nature Switzerland AG 2022
S. Bhalachandra et al. (Eds.): WACCPD 2021, LNCS 13194, pp. 73–91, 2022.
https://doi.org/10.1007/978-3-030-97759-7_4

1 Introduction

The variety of applications in the HPC field is increasing in recent years, including not only applications based on the conventional equation-based method, but also those based on the data-driven method and those based on the combination of the equation-based method and the data-driven method. In addition, the variety of computer architecture is increasing in a wide range of systems from commodity to supercomputer systems (e.g., x86/Arm/Power CPUs and NVIDIA/AMD/Intel GPUs). It is a challenge to make applications executable in multiple computer systems with low development cost and sufficient performance for making effective use of various computer architectures in these various applications.

Aiming to achieve performance portability among multiple architectures with small development cost, directive-based parallel programming models that enable porting of code across parallel environments via addition of directives to CPU code have been developed. Using OpenACC [8], which is a type of directive-based parallel programming model, many equation-based applications have been successfully ported to GPU systems (e.g., [10,14,15,17,19]), and some studies report performance similar to that based on native programming models (e.g., [20] reported performance similar to that using CUDA on NVIDIA GPUs). On the other hand, there are only a few examples demonstrating the effectiveness of the directive-based programming model for a wider variety of applications combining data-driven and equation-based methods. Therefore, in this paper, we show that directive based parallel programming is effective even in recent diverse applications by porting applications that combine data-driven and equation-based methods to GPU by OpenACC.

In this study, we focus on a neural network (NN)-accelerated implicit solver [13], which incorporates the data-driven method into the equation-based method to accelerate a partial differential equation (PDE) solver. In this method, the problem of insufficient accuracy of the data-driven method, which often arises when combining the data-driven method with equation-based methods, is solved by developing a preconditioner that uses NNs via Green's function (GF) that reflects the characteristics of the target PDE (GF-based NN preconditioner). Since the sparse calculation and random data access involved in the PDE solver was transferred to NNs with compute efficient dense calculation and continuous data access, the NN-accelerated solver was 4.26 times faster than the conventional PDE-based solver on CPU systems. As the calculations in the preconditioner are spatially localized, high scalability was attained in the massively parallel environment of Fugaku [2]. This solver algorithm is expected to be effective in a wide range of recent computer architectures; high-efficiency on GPUs is expected by development of kernel algorithms and implementations suitable for recent GPU architecture.

The rest of the paper is organized as below. Section 2 outlines the GF-based NN preconditioned implicit solver that is the subject of this study. Section 3 explains how to port the solver to the GPU. Here, kernel algorithms suitable for the target GPU architecture are built based on the scalable solver algorithm, and the application is implemented using OpenACC. The performance of the development method is shown in Sect. 4. Here, kernel performance on GPUs are measured for kernel algorithms designed for CPUs and that designed for GPUs. The performance of kernels implemented using CUDA, which has a high implementation cost but high specializability, is also shown to discuss the performance portability when using low-implementation cost methods such as OpenACC for GPU-based acceleration. Section 5 summarizes the paper.

2 Solver with Green's Function-Based NN Preconditioner

As an example of a neural network (NN)-accelerated implicit solver, we target a Green's function-based NN preconditioned implicit solver, which uses NNs via Green's function that reflects the characteristics of the target PDE as a predictor in the preconditioner of an iterative solver [13]. Below, we describe the target PDE, GF-based NN predictor, the algorithm of utilizing this NN in the implicit solver.

2.1 Target Problem

As an example of PDE-based physics simulation, we target wave propagation in a domain with heterogeneous material properties

$$\rho \frac{\partial^2 u_i}{\partial t^2} = \frac{\partial}{\partial x_j} \left(c_{ijkl} \frac{\partial u_k}{\partial x_l} \right) + f_i. \tag{1}$$

Here, x, t, ρ, u, c, f indicate coordinates, time, density, displacement, elasticity tensor, and outer force, respectively. For simplicity, voxel finite elements with Newmark-β ($\beta = 1/4, \gamma = 1/2$) implicit time integration is used for discretization of Eq. (1). The target problem becomes

$$\mathbf{A}\delta\mathbf{u} = \mathbf{f}, \tag{2}$$

where

$$\mathbf{A} = \frac{4}{dt^2}\mathbf{M} + \frac{2}{dt}\mathbf{C}^n + \mathbf{K}^n, \tag{3}$$

$$\mathbf{f} = \mathbf{b}^n - \mathbf{q}^{n-1} + \mathbf{C}^n\mathbf{v}^{n-1} + \mathbf{A}\left(\mathbf{a}^{n-1} + \frac{4}{dt}\mathbf{v}^{n-1}\right). \tag{4}$$

Here, superscript n indicates the time step number, dt indicates time step increment, and $\mathbf{M}, \mathbf{C}^n, \mathbf{K}^n$, indicate mass, damping, and stiffness matrices, respectively. Using the displacement increment $\delta\mathbf{u}$ obtained by solving Eq. (2), displacement, velocity, acceleration, and inner force are updated as

$$\mathbf{u}^n = \mathbf{u}^{n-1} + \delta\mathbf{u},$$

$$\mathbf{v}^n = -\mathbf{v}^{n-1} + \frac{2}{dt}\delta\mathbf{u},$$

$$\mathbf{a}^n = -\mathbf{a}^{n-1} - \frac{4}{dt}\mathbf{v}^{n-1} + \frac{4}{dt^2}\delta\mathbf{u},$$

$$\mathbf{q}^n = \mathbf{q}^{n-1} + \mathbf{K}^n\delta\mathbf{u}.$$

The problems targeted in this study become larger than 10^9 degrees of freedom (DOF); thus, accelerating the solver in solving Eq. (2) with 10^9 DOF becomes the target problem.

2.2   GF-Based NN Predictor

Since the accuracy of the results of data-driven methods such as NNs are not always guaranteed, we use the NNs as a predictor in the preconditioning process of the iterative solution method instead of using NN for directly obtaining the solution of Eq. (2). In order for this solver to be faster than solvers based on conventional equation-based methods, it is important to gain accuracy more efficiently (i.e., reduce the cost per accuracy) than the preconditioners in the equation-based method. The most straight forward way to use a NN as a predictor is to build a surrogate model that reproduces the behavior of the entire system using NN, and this approach has been shown to be effective in small-scale problems [12,16]. On the other hand, in a large-scale problem, not only the number of modes increases, but also the data representing each mode (i.e., set of $(\mathbf{x}, \mathbf{Ax})$) becomes large. Thus, using this approach for obtaining high accuracy behavior of the entire system incurs huge cost for large-scale problems. Therefore, we obtain highly accurate estimation with low cost by constructing a local NN via a GF that reflects the characteristics of PDE. Below, we explain the method of generating GF-based NN.

For a PDE

$$L(x)(a(x)) = b(x), \tag{5}$$

the Green's function of this PDE is defined as $g(x, s)$ that satisfies

$$L(g(x, s)) = \delta(s - x). \tag{6}$$

Here, L, b, a, δ indicate the linear differential operator, known distribution, response of system, and the Dirac delta function, respectively. By using this Green's function, response of system can be obtained explicitly as

$$a(x) = \int g(x, s)b(s)\mathrm{d}s. \tag{7}$$

In this way, GF reflects the characteristics of PDE, and linear equations can be solved immediately by convolution calculation. However, the GF approach is rarely used because the calculation to obtain the discretized distribution of GFs costs the same as the calculation to solve the linear equations discretized from PDE. Therefore, in this research, we solve the problem of GF cost and the problem of accuracy when using NNs by estimating GFs in a short time with NNs as follows.

Since the target domain comprises heterogeneous materials, the distribution of GF will also change according to the material property distribution. The discretized GF has a complicated distribution as shown in Fig. 1; thus, it is difficult to efficiently estimate its distribution up to higher-order modes with a small amount of data. Therefore, GFs in domains with heterogeneous material properties are calculated via the following two steps assuming that the GFs can be approximated by using a simple transformation of the distribution of the GF in a domain with homogeneous material properties.

1. Select one physical property value that represents the heterogeneous material property, and obtain the discretized GF in the homogeneous region with this material property. Since the Green's function of the wave equation decreases with distance, the GF value in the region of the $N_x \times N_y \times N_z$ nodes where the GF has a significant value is obtained (the values outside of this region are neglected). Here, the wave velocities (V_s, V_p), discretization width (ds, dt), and cutoff criteria automatically determine the value N_x, N_y, N_z. Here, we use data sets comprising $(\mathbf{x}, \mathbf{Ax})$, $\mathbf{x}$ is a random input field, for numerical optimization for obtaining the distribution of GF at the $N_x \times N_y \times N_z$ nodes.

2. Next, we construct an NN that maps the GF in the homogeneous material region to the GF in the heterogeneous material property region. Here, we assume that the nine components of GF $\mathbf{G}_{ij}(i, j = 1, 2, 3)$ can be approximated as

$$\mathbf{G}_{ii}^{NN} = \mathbf{G}_{ii}^{base}(c_1 + c_2 x + c_3 y + c_4 z), \tag{8}$$

$$\mathbf{G}_{ij}^{NN} = \mathbf{G}_{ij}^{base}(c_5 + c_6 x + c_7 y + c_8 z) \quad \text{for} \quad i \neq j, \tag{9}$$

using eight coefficients c_i $(i = 1, 2, ..., 8)$ obtained using NNs. Note that the nine components of GF are approximated with two sets of four coefficients, as an isotropic material is targeted. Here, NNs inputting material properties of $(N_x-1) \times (N_y-1) \times (N_z-1)$ elements and outputting values of $c_i(i = 1, 2, ..., 8)$ are used. Classifier NNs using fully connected 8-4-4-4-4-4-25 feed-forward networks based on Chainer are used [4].

This makes it possible to construct an NN that estimates GF with high accuracy with a small amount of data and a small number of parameters, as compared with the case of directly estimating GF in the heterogeneous material property domain. Figure 1 shows the distribution of GF estimated using NN constructed using 16.2 million sets of data for training ($N_x = N_y = N_z = 7$; the number of input material property parameters is $6^3 = 216$, and the output value of GF is $7^3 \times 9$ components. The upper part of the figure is the accurate GF, and the lower part is the error of GF estimated by the developed NNs. Here, we plot the results for the performance measurement problem shown in Sect. 5. From the figure, we can see that although each component of GF has a complicated higher-order mode, each component of GF in a region with different material properties can be obtained with high accuracy.

Using the obtained $\mathbf{G}_{ij}^{NN}(i, j = 1, 2, 3)$, the solution to equation $\mathbf{Az} = \mathbf{r}$ is approximated as

$$z_i(i_x, i_y, i_z) = \sum_{j=1}^{3} \sum_{j_z=1}^{N_z} \sum_{j_y=1}^{N_y} \sum_{j_x=1}^{N_x} \{G_{ij}^{NN}(j_x, j_y, j_z)$$

$$r_j(i_x + j_x - N_x/2, i_y + j_y - N_y/2, i_z + j_z - N_z/2)\} \quad \text{for } i = 1, 2, 3, \tag{10}$$

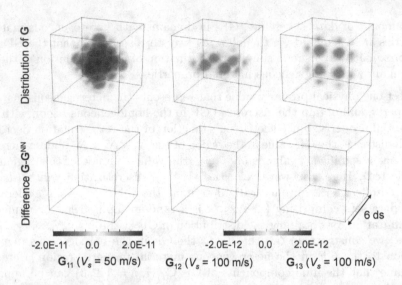

Fig. 1. Accuracy of GFs obtained by NNs. Upper row indicate the true values, while the lower row indicate the errors of the NN-approximated values.

where $z_i(i_x, i_y, i_z)$ denotes the i-th component of $\mathbf{z}$ at voxel node at position i_x, i_y, i_z, and $G_{ij}^{NN}(j_x, j_y, j_z)$ indicates the i,j component of the approximated Green's function at position j_x, j_y, j_z.

2.3   Scalable Solver Algorithm Using GF-Based NN Predictor

We develop a scalable solver algorithm by incorporating the GF-based NN into the adaptive conjugate gradient method [11]. In the normal preconditioning method of CG solvers, the search direction $\mathbf{z} = \mathbf{Mr}$ is calculated using a fixed matrix $\mathbf{M}$ that approximates $\mathbf{A}^{-1}$. However, in the adaptive conjugate gradient method, $\mathbf{z}$ obtained by approximately solving $\mathbf{Az} = \mathbf{r}$, is used in the search direction. This enables using the GF-based NN predictor, which is an inexact calculation, in the preconditioner of an iterative solver. Below we describe the algorithm following Algorithm 1.

– Preconditioner: As the distribution of GF changes significantly in the boundary region, the GF-based NN predictor is used to predict $\mathbf{z} = \mathbf{A}^{-1}\mathbf{r}$ in domains distant from the boundaries (Algorithm 1 line 8), and parts near boundaries are updated by roughly solving the equation using a standard CG solver (Algorithm 1 line 9). In addition, in order to avoid communication required for GF calculation at the domain boundary in MPI process partition boundaries, these parts are also updated by the CG method together with the physical domain boundaries. When updating these boundary areas, we use the memory-saving and highly scalable 3×3 block Jacobi preconditioned CG method.

Algorithm 1. Iterative solver with NN-based preconditioner for solving Eq. (2). Here, GF-based NNs ($\mathbf{Br}$ is the estimation of the solution of equation $\mathbf{Az} = \mathbf{r}$ by the NNs) is used in the preconditioner in an adaptive conjugate gradient method. Matrix vector product of $\mathbf{A}$ and $\mathbf{A}_p$ are computed by the EBE method. ($^-$) and ϵ indicates single-precision variable and tolerance for relative error. As the GF-based NNs are highly accurate and capable of resolving high frequency modes, high refinement rate is expected in the iterative solution refinement.

1: $\mathbf{r} \Leftarrow \mathbf{f} - \mathbf{A}\delta\mathbf{u}$
2: $\beta \Leftarrow 0$
3: $i \Leftarrow 1$
4: (* outer loop start *)
5: **while** $\|\mathbf{r}\|_2/\|\mathbf{f}\|_2 \geq \epsilon$ **do**
6:     (* preconditioner start *)
7:     $\bar{\mathbf{r}} \Leftarrow \mathbf{r}$
8:     $\bar{\mathbf{z}} \Leftarrow \bar{\mathbf{B}}\bar{\mathbf{r}}$ (* apply GF-based NNs inside process domain *)
9:     $\bar{\mathbf{z}}_p \Leftarrow \bar{\mathbf{A}}_p^{-1}\bar{\mathbf{r}}_p$ (* refine solution near domain boundary and inter-process boundary using conjugate gradient solver with 3×3 block Jacobi preconditioning up to ϵ_p with Dirichlet boundary conditions with value of $\bar{\mathbf{z}}$ and initial solution $\bar{\mathbf{z}}_p = \mathbf{0}$ elsewhere *)
10:     $\mathbf{z} \Leftarrow \bar{\mathbf{z}}$ using $\bar{\mathbf{z}}$ updated with $\bar{\mathbf{z}}_p$
11:     (* preconditioner end *)
12:     **if** $i > 1$ **then**
13:         $\beta \Leftarrow (\mathbf{z}, \mathbf{q})/\rho$
14:     **end if**
15:     $\mathbf{p} \Leftarrow \mathbf{z} + \beta\mathbf{p}$
16:     $\mathbf{q} \Leftarrow \mathbf{Ap}$
17:     $\rho \Leftarrow (\mathbf{z}, \mathbf{r})$
18:     $\alpha \Leftarrow \rho/(\mathbf{p}, \mathbf{q})$
19:     $\mathbf{r} \Leftarrow \mathbf{r} - \alpha\mathbf{q}$
20:     $\delta\mathbf{u} \Leftarrow \delta\mathbf{u} + \alpha\mathbf{p}$
21:     $i \Leftarrow i + 1$
22: **end while**
23: (* outer loop end *)

– Matrix-free matrix-vector product: In order to conduct large-scale computation on systems with a limited amount of memory, the matrix-vector product $\mathbf{f} = \mathbf{Au}$ is calculated without storing the entire matrix $\mathbf{A}$, which uses a lot of memory, in memory. Here, using the Element-by-Element method [18], the product of the element matrix $\mathbf{A}_e$ and the element right-side vector $\mathbf{u}_e$ is calculated and added to the entire left-side vector $\mathbf{f}$ each time a matrix-vector product is calculated. Since it is possible to reduce not only the memory usage but also the memory transfer amount as compared with the case of storing the entire matrix, this algorithm is suitable for systems with relatively high computational performance in comparison with respect the memory bandwidth. The EBE method is used for the matrix-vector product at line 16 of

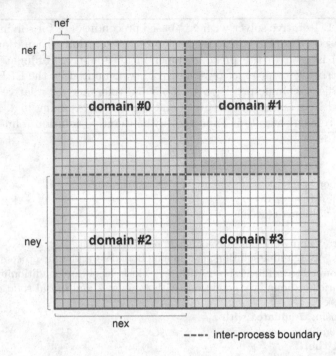

Fig. 2. Using GF-based NN predictor. White parts are predicted by GF-based NN while the colored parts near inter-process boundary and physical domain boundaries are solved roughly using a conjugate gradient solver. $\mathtt{nef} = 3$ is used in this study.

Algorithm 1 and matrix-vector products within the CG method for updating the boundary part in line 9 of Algorithm 1.
- Mixed precision arithmetic: Although the final output of the calculation requires double precision, the preconditioning calculation can be inexact; thus, the computation involved in preconditioning is conducted in single precision (computation except for the preconditioner is conducted in double precision). Not only high-peak performance hardware can be used, but the amount of intra-process data movement and inter-process communication can be halved.

3 GPU Porting of Solver with Green's Function-Based NN Preconditioner Using OpenACC

The GF-based NN preconditioned solver algorithm, which comprises the data-driven modeling part (GF-based NN-predictor) and equation-based modeling part (other solver components), is expected to perform well on a wide range of architectures, including GPUs, because of its dense NN computation and structured data access. On the other hand, at the kernel level, there are some

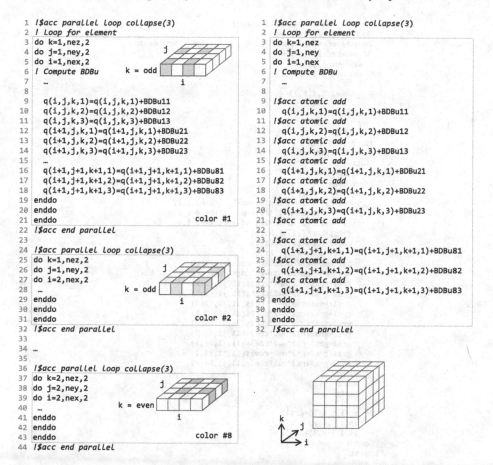

```
1  !$acc parallel loop collapse(3)
2  ! Loop for element
3  do k=1,nez,2
4  do j=1,ney,2
5  do i=1,nex,2
6  ! Compute BDBu          k = odd
7  ...
8
9     q(i,j,k,1)=q(i,j,k,1)+BDBu11
10    q(i,j,k,2)=q(i,j,k,2)+BDBu12
11    q(i,j,k,3)=q(i,j,k,3)+BDBu13
12    q(i+1,j,k,1)=q(i+1,j,k,1)+BDBu21
13    q(i+1,j,k,2)=q(i+1,j,k,2)+BDBu22
14    q(i+1,j,k,3)=q(i+1,j,k,3)+BDBu23
15    ...
16    q(i+1,j+1,k+1,1)=q(i+1,j+1,k+1,1)+BDBu81
17    q(i+1,j+1,k+1,2)=q(i+1,j+1,k+1,2)+BDBu82
18    q(i+1,j+1,k+1,3)=q(i+1,j+1,k+1,3)+BDBu83
19 enddo
20 enddo
21 enddo                          color #1
22 !$acc end parallel
23
24 !$acc parallel loop collapse(3)
25 do k=1,nez,2
26 do j=1,ney,2
27 do i=2,nex,2
28 ...                   k = odd
29 enddo
30 enddo
31 enddo                          color #2
32 !$acc end parallel
33
34 ...
35
36 !$acc parallel loop collapse(3)
37 do k=2,nez,2
38 do j=2,ney,2
39 do i=2,nex,2
40 ...                  k = even
41 enddo
42 enddo
43 enddo                          color #8
44 !$acc end parallel
```

```
1  !$acc parallel loop collapse(3)
2  ! Loop for element
3  do k=1,nez
4  do j=1,ney
5  do i=1,nex
6  ! Compute BDBu
7  ...
8
9  !$acc atomic add
10    q(i,j,k,1)=q(i,j,k,1)+BDBu11
11 !$acc atomic add
12    q(i,j,k,2)=q(i,j,k,2)+BDBu12
13 !$acc atomic add
14    q(i,j,k,3)=q(i,j,k,3)+BDBu13
15 !$acc atomic add
16    q(i+1,j,k,1)=q(i+1,j,k,1)+BDBu21
17 !$acc atomic add
18    q(i+1,j,k,2)=q(i+1,j,k,2)+BDBu22
19 !$acc atomic add
20    q(i+1,j,k,3)=q(i+1,j,k,3)+BDBu23
21 !$acc atomic add
22    ...
23 !$acc atomic add
24    q(i+1,j+1,k+1,1)=q(i+1,j+1,k+1,1)+BDBu81
25 !$acc atomic add
26    q(i+1,j+1,k+1,2)=q(i+1,j+1,k+1,2)+BDBu82
27 !$acc atomic add
28    q(i+1,j+1,k+1,3)=q(i+1,j+1,k+1,3)+BDBu83
29 enddo
30 enddo
31 enddo
32 !$acc end parallel
```

Fig. 3. Avoiding data recurrence in the matrix-vector product kernel. Left: Using coloring of elements, right: using atomic add.

algorithms that perform well on GPUs and others that do not, so appropriate algorithm selection is necessary at the kernel level. In this study, we developed a kernel algorithm suitable for GPU architectures by reducing reading from and writing to GPU memory and coalesced access to make effective use of bandwidth. In addition, since GPUs tend to have communication bottlenecks due to their high computing power, we also reduce communication between MPI processes. Note that all computation is offloaded to the GPU, and the CPU is used only to manage the GPU[1]. In the following, we describe the kernel algorithm and implementation suitable for GPUs for the main kernels.

---

[1] Since implicit data transfer between CPU and GPU is conducted every time in acc parallel/kernels region by default in OpenACC, all necessary variables are copied into GPU memory in advance, and only the minimum necessary acc update host/device is used in the offloaded region.

```
1  !$acc parallel loop collapse(3)
2  do k=1+nef-1,nez+1-nef+1
3  do j=1+nef-1,ney+1-nef+1              SIMT computation
4  do i=1+nef-1,nex+1-nef+1
5    we1=wei(i,j,k,1)
6    we2=wei(i,j,k,2)
7    …
8    we8=wei(i,j,k,8)
9
10   grs1=0.
11   grs2=0.
12   grs3=0.
13 !$acc loop seq
14   do k1=1,nd*2+1
15 !$acc loop seq
16   do i1=1,nd*2+1
17 !$acc loop seq
18   do j1=1,nd*2+1
19     rs1=rs(i1+i-nd-1,j1+j-nd-1,k1+k-nd-1,1)
20     rs2=rs(i1+i-nd-1,j1+j-nd-1,k1+k-nd-1,2)
21     rs3=rs(i1+i-nd-1,j1+j-nd-1,k1+k-nd-1,3)
22     cocs1=cocs(i1,j1,k1,1)
23     cocs2=cocs(i1,j1,k1,2)
24     cocs3=cocs(i1,j1,k1,3)
25     ww1=we1+we2*cocs1+we3*cocs2+we4*cocs3
26     ww2=we5+we6*cocs1+we7*cocs2+we8*cocs3
27     grs1=grs1+rs1*ww1*coe1s(i1,j1,k1,1)
28     grs1=grs1+rs2*ww2*coe1s(i1,j1,k1,2)
29     grs1=grs1+rs3*ww2*coe1s(i1,j1,k1,3)
30     grs2=grs2+rs1*ww2*coe2s(i1,j1,k1,1)
31     grs2=grs2+rs2*ww1*coe2s(i1,j1,k1,2)
32     grs2=grs2+rs3*ww2*coe2s(i1,j1,k1,3)
33     grs3=grs3+rs1*ww2*coe3s(i1,j1,k1,1)
34     grs3=grs3+rs2*ww2*coe3s(i1,j1,k1,2)
35     grs3=grs3+rs3*ww1*coe3s(i1,j1,k1,3)
36   enddo
37   enddo
38   enddo
39
40   zs(i,j,k,1)=grs1
41   zs(i,j,k,2)=grs2
42   zs(i,j,k,3)=grs3
43 enddo
44 enddo
45 enddo
46 !$acc parallel loop collapse(3)
```

Fig. 4. GF-based NN predictor kernel

– Avoiding data recurrence in matrix-vector product kernel: In parallel computation of matrix-vector product kernels, it is necessary to avoid the data recurrence that occurs when adding to the left-side vector. The simplest way is coloring the elements into eight different colors as shown in the left part of Fig. 3. Focusing on a single voxel element, the number of nodes to be added is eight, so by coloring the region with different eight colors so that each element doesn't share nodes with each other, we can avoid race condition within each color. In the left part of Fig. 3, each code segment represents each of the eight colors. This method is simple and can be used on GPUs running many threads, but it results in stride 2 data access. Recent GPUs often equip hardware-accelerated atomics; in particular, recent NVIDIA GPUs have high throughput atomic operations capability, so we can expect performance improvement by avoiding data recurrence using this feature. As shown in the right part of Fig. 3, by utilizing atomic add, stride 2 data access in the coloring algorithm is replaced by continuous access, which is expected to improve performance on GPUs with fast atomics.

- Element wise computation in matrix-vector product kernel: Since recent GPUs have a large number of registers per thread, shorter elapsed time tends to be achieved by reducing data access even if the amount of computation on registers is increased. Therefore, the kernel algorithm that previously calculated intermediate variables and stored in memory are changed such that these variables are recalculated every time on the fly on GPUs. This reduces the amount of GPU memory read in the matrix-vector product kernel, which is expected to lead to speedup.
- GF-based NN predictor kernel: This kernel computes the convolution of the information of the surrounding grid into local nodes, and has a simple loop structure with a triple loop within a triple loop as shown in Fig. 4. To make effective use of the large number of threads on the GPU, the outer triple loop is collapsed to make the loop length long enough for parallelization. Also, the array dimensions of variables to be read in the kernel are set appropriately, so that all data accesses become coalesced accesses. Furthermore, by unrolling the outermost loop for k, the variables loaded in the innermost loop can be reused for further performance increase.
- Mapping of processes for efficient communication: Recent GPU compute nodes are often equipped with multiple GPUs and multiple communication ports; thus, it is important to reduce inter-node communication and effectively utilize communication bandwidth by allocating processes and communication ports according to these configurations. In this case, we adopt the process mapping as shown in Fig. 5, considering an environment where the communication between GPUs in a node is faster than the communication between nodes, and where the transfer rate between GPUs and communication ports in a node is nonuniform. The process mapping is arranged in such a way that the communication ports close to each GPU are used and the amount of communication in each port is balanced. The above mapping was created for the configuration of the compute nodes of the 2D process partitioning and ABCI supercomputer system used for performance measurement in this research, but appropriate mappings can be created for other configurations and 3D process partitioning as well.

4   Performance Measurement

4.1   Problem Used for Measurement

As an example of a large-scale wave propagation analysis in a domain with heterogeneous material properties, we measure the performance of the wave propagation analysis in a head model [9] created by a CT scan (Fig. 6), following the performance measurement problem in [13]. Here, V_s takes a value between 50 m/s and 120 m/s, and other material properties are fixed at damping $h = 0.001$, density $\rho = 1000$ kg/m^3, and $V_p = 200$ m/s. The problem is discretized in the time

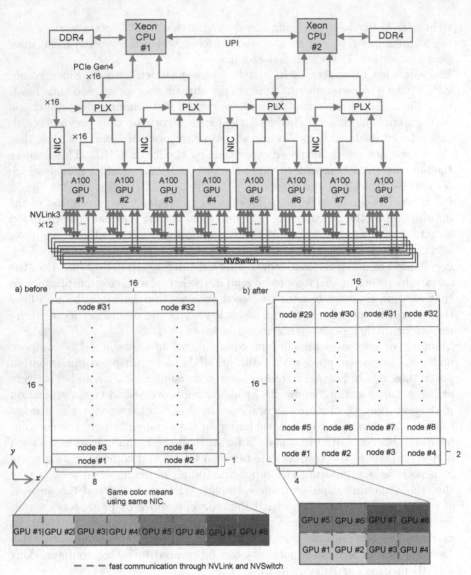

Fig. 5. Diagram of compute node (A) of ABCI [1] and Mapping of processes for efficient communication. (top) Each GPU is connected to each other via NVLink and NVSwitch, allowing them to communicate with each other at high speed in each compute node. (bottom) Here, this is a mapping of processes for a system comprising compute nodes each with 8 GPUs and 4 NICs shown in above image. By using b) instead of a), maximum inter-node communication volume can be reduced by 40% per NIC.

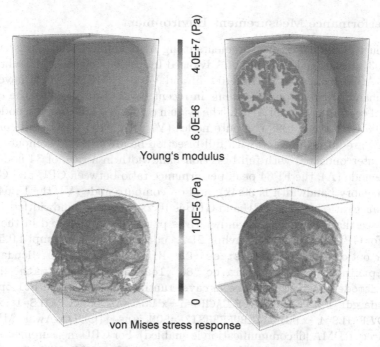

Fig. 6. Head model used for performance measurement. Young's modulus and von Mises stress response of the model under gravity is shown.

with $dt = 0.001$ s and space is divided into $512 \times 512 \times 512$ in the x, y, and z directions by voxel elements ($513 \times 513 \times 513$ nodes, 3 degrees of freedom in x, y, z directions per node for a total of 405,017,091 DOF). When measuring weak scaling, this head model is duplicated in the x, y directions. Since the convergence properties of the iterative solver do not change significantly in the time direction as a linear problem is solved, we measure the time required to solve one time step with $\mathbf{f}$ with white noise and clamped boundary condition at the bottom of the model. The cost of constructing NN is small and can be built in advance, so only the solver part including the inference by NN is measured.

In this study, we compare performance of the developed solver with CGBJ (conjugate gradient method with 3×3-block Jacobi preconditioning), which is a kind of equation based solver widely used for solving large-scale wave problems in massively parallel environments. CGBJ has good load balance because it uses the inverse matrix calculated locally for each node for preconditioning. In addition, since CGBJ consists only of matrix-vector products, it can be implemented in a memory-saving manner by combining it with the Element-by-Element method, making it a suitable method for solving large-scale problems. In this study, the CGBJ is implemented by substituting the GF-based NN predictor in lines 6–11 in Algorithm 1 with a 3×3-block Jacobi preconditioner; thus, the CGBJ solver is implemented in the same level as in the developed solver.

4.2 Performance Measurement Environment

We conduct performance measurements using AI Bridging Cloud Infrastructure (ABCI) [3] at National Institute of Advanced Industrial Science and Technology (AIST). ABCI equips NVIDIA A100 [5] and V100 [7] GPUs, which have been used in many supercomputer systems in recent years. Table 1 shows the configuration of compute nodes of ABCI. The system comprises 120 compute nodes (A) with A100 GPUs and 1088 compute nodes (V) with V100 GPUs. All compute nodes (A) are interconnected with full bisection bandwidth and compute nodes (V) are interconnected with full bisection bandwidth in a rack of 34 nodes. On compute node (A), the FP64 peak performance ratio between CPU and GPU is 14.0x (memory bandwidth is 30.4x), and on compute node (V), the FP64 peak performance ratio between CPU and GPU is 10.2x (memory bandwidth is 14.1x). We can see that the memory bandwidth is particularly enhanced in the A100 nodes. For GPU measurements, nvhpc 21.2, cuda 11.2.2, and openmpi 4.0.5, with compiler options `-fopenmp -fastsse -O3 -Minline=levels:10 -Mcuda=cuda "11.2",ptxinfo -acc -ta=tesla:cc "80",loadcache:L1,fastmath -Minfo= accel -mcmodel=medium -Mlarge_arrays`, runtime options `--mca btl_openib_ want_cuda_gdr 1 x UCX_MEMTYPE_CACHE=n -x UCX_MAX_EAGER_RAILS=1 -x UCX_ MAX_RNDV_RAILS=1 -x PGI_ACC_BUFFERSIZE=50M`, is used (CUDA-Aware MPI and GPU Direct RDMA [6] communication is enabled). For CPU measurements, intel 2020.4.304, intel-mpi 2019.9, with compiler options `-O3 -xCORE-AVX512 -qopenmp -qopt-report -qopt-zmm-usage=high`, is used. All CPU cores in a node are used with OpenMP (9 cores/process in compute node (A), 10 cores/process in compute node (V)). An implementation tuned with SIMD intrinsics (AVX-512) developed in [13] is used for measurements on CPUs. In the following measurements, we fix the problem size to $256 \times 256 \times 512$ elements per process (1 GPU per process).

Table 1. Configuration of ABCI system

Compute node (A)		Hardware peak per node
CPU	Intel Xeon Platinum 8360Y	5.529 TFLOPS
	(2.40 GHz, 36 Cores) ×2	
Memory	512 GB DDR4 3200 MHz RDIMM	408 GB/s
GPU	NVIDIA A100 NVLink	77.6 TFLOPS
	40 GB HBM2 ×8	12.4 TB/s
Interconnect	InfiniBand HDR (200 Gbps) ×4	100 GB/s
Compute node (V)		Hardware peak per node
CPU	Intel Xeon Gold 6148	3.072 TFLOPS
	(2.40 GHz, 20 Cores) ×2	
Memory	384 GB DDR4 2666 MHz RDIMM	256 GB/s
GPU	NVIDIA V100 SXM2	31.2 TFLOPS
	16 GB HBM2 ×4	3.6 TB/s
Interconnect	InfiniBand EDR (100 Gbps) ×2	25 GB/s

4.3 Solver Performance on GPU-Based System

First, we measure the performance of the developed method at the kernel level (Table 2).

– EBE kernel: Since this kernel has many intermediate variables and data access, spill/fill occurred on CPUs with a limited number of registers, resulting in a peak performance of 11.2% to the FP64 peak. On the other hand, on GPUs, spill/fill is avoided due to the large number of registers, resulting in a high peak performance ratio. First, for the coloring algorithm shown in the left side of Fig. 3, the performance of the EBE kernel is 28.2 ms, 5.33 TFLOPS (55% of the FP64 peak performance ratio), which is higher than that of the CPU. Algorithm in the right side of Fig. 3 making effective use of atomics resulted in 21.5 ms, 6.99 TFLOPS (72% of FP64 peak performance), which is 1.31 times faster than that of coloring. Furthermore, the use of an algorithm that reduces memory read by recalculation of intermediate variables led to a 93.7-fold speedup compared to the CPU (75.0% of peak performance).
– GF-based NN predictor kernel: Due to the high compute density and small data access, the CPU implementation has a high performance of 35.3% of the FP32 peak performance ratio, but the A100 GPU implementation has an even higher performance (9.63 TFLOPS, equivalent to 49.4% of the FP32 peak performance ratio). This can be attributed to the effective hiding of data access and arithmetic latency by use of the large number of threads and registers.

As can be seen, both the EBE kernel and GF-based NN predictor kernel are significantly faster than the CPU implementation. With these kernel-level speedups, the entire solver is 38.9-fold faster than the CPU implementation on the A100 node (Table 2) and 22.4-fold faster than the CPU implementation on the V100 node (Table 3).

Table 2. Performance of proposed solver on compute node (A) × 1 node

On CPU (2 36-core Xeon CPUs)	Elapsed time	TFLOPS (peak ratio)	
GF-based NN predictor (FP32)	4.83 s	1.95 ×2 (35.3% to FP32 peak)	
Boundary part EBE (FP32)	3.19 s	0.69 ×2 (12.5% to FP32 peak)	
Outer EBE (FP64)	11.62 s	0.31 ×2 (11.2% to FP64 peak)	
Total (mixed-precision)	23.96 s	0.64 ×2 (23.1% to FP64 peak)	
On GPU (8 A100 GPUs)	Elapsed time	TFLOPS (peak ratio)	Speedup
GF-based NN predictor (FP32)	0.246 s	9.63 ×8 (49.4% to FP32 peak)	19.6
Boundary part EBE (FP32)	0.042 s	13.2 ×8 (07.5% to FP32 peak)	75.9
Outer EBE (FP64)	0.124 s	7.27 ×8 (75.0% to FP64 peak)	93.7
Total (mixed-precision)	0.612 s	6.25 ×8 (64.4% to FP64 peak)	38.9

Table 3. Performance of proposed solver on compute node (V) × 2 nodes

On CPU (4 20-core Xeon CPUs)	Elapsed time	TFLOPS (peak ratio)	
GF-based NN predictor (FP32)	5.17 s	0.91 ×4 (29.7% to FP32 peak)	
Boundary part EBE (FP32)	2.76 s	0.40 ×4 (15.0% to FP32 peak)	
Outer EBE (FP64)	9.75 s	0.74 ×4 (18.5% to FP64 peak)	
Total (mixed-precision)	20.9 s	0.37 ×4 (23.9% to FP64 peak)	
On GPU (8 V100 GPUs)	Elapsed time	TFLOPS (peak ratio)	Speedup
GF-based NN predictor (FP32)	0.332 s	7.12 ×8 (45.4% to FP32 peak)	15.6
Boundary part EBE (FP32)	0.062 s	8.93 ×8 (56.9% to FP32 peak)	44.2
Outer EBE (FP64)	0.173 s	5.23 ×8 (67.0% to FP64 peak)	56.3
Total (mixed-precision)	0.933 s	4.10 ×8 (52.6% to FP64 peak)	22.4

Compared to the CUDA implementation, which is more expensive to implement but offers greater programming flexibility, the outer EBE kernel and GF-based NN predictor kernel on the A100 node achieved 93.0% and 85.5% of the performance implemented by CUDA, respectively. On the V100 node, the performance of the Outer EBE kernel and GF-based NN predictor kernel was 91.8% and 82.7% of the performance implemented by CUDA, respectively. Thus, by designing an algorithm that is suitable for GPUs, we can see that the performance of the OpenACC implementation is comparable to that of the CUDA implementation in practical use.

Next we compare the performance of the developed solver with the standard equation-based solver CGBJ (3 × 3 block Jacobi CG method). From Fig. 7, we can see that while CGBJ required 42 iterations, the developed method required only 5 iterations to solve the equation up to a relative error $|\mathbf{A}\delta\mathbf{u} - \mathbf{b}|/|\mathbf{b}| < 10^{-8}$. From this, we can see that the accuracy of the predictor is higher than that of the conventional equation-based preconditioner used in CGBJ. The GF-based NN predictor can also be used for initial solution estimation as indicated as "NN initial solution + CGBJ" in Fig. 7. However, the performance improvement is small in this case; we can see that using GF-based NN for solution refinement via a preconditioner is important for attaining performance. When this problem is measured on the A100 node system, one iteration of the GF-based solver required only about 2.68 times that of one CGBJ iteration, which lead to 2.54-fold speedup of the entire solver. The reduction in the number of iterations by the high-accuracy predictor, and the peak performance ratio improved from 41.9% of CGBJ to 64.4% in the proposed method by NNs, lead to the speedup.

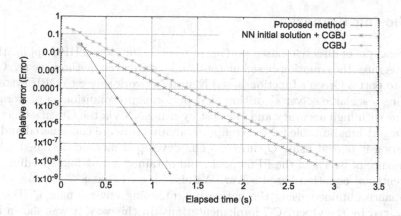

Fig. 7. Comparison of the performance of solver algorithms. Elapsed time on compute node (A) system is shown in the horizontal axis.

Table 4. Weak scaling of proposed solver on compute node (A) system.

# of nodes	# of GPUs	Solver total elapsed time (s)	Point-to-point comm. time (s)	Others time (s)	Scalability
1	8	0.624	0.007	0.617	-
2	16	0.642	0.021	0.620	97.1%
4	32	0.725	0.054	0.671	86.0%
8	64	0.741	0.061	0.679	84.2%
16	128	0.738	0.058	0.679	84.5%
32	256	0.748	0.062	0.685	83.4%

4.4   Weak Scaling on GPU-Based System

Finally, we measure the scalability of the proposed method on large scale problems. Here, we fix the problem size to $256 \times 256 \times 512$ elements per process (1 GPU) and scale up the number of processes and the problem size. Table 4 shows the performance from 1 node (8 GPUs) to 32 nodes (256 GPUs) on the A100 node system. From the table, we can see that the time required for point-to-point communication increases from 1 to 4 nodes, but remains almost constant for more than 4 nodes. This is thought to be due to the characteristics of the full bisection network, which allows for efficient neighbor-node communications. As a result, high weak scaling efficiency of 83.4% was achieved from 1 node (8 GPUs) to 32 nodes (256 GPUs). We can see that the well maintained load balancing and the preconditioner with reduced communication lead to high performance on a parallel environment comprising a large number of GPUs.

5   Closing Remarks

As an example of directive-based porting of recently developed HPC applications that integrates the equation-based method and data-driven method, we use OpenACC to port a Green's function-based Neural Network solver to GPU systems. Targeting a scalable solver algorithm that performs preconditioning of iterative solutions with high accuracy and low cost by using NN via the Green's function, kernel algorithms suitable for the computer architecture are constructed and the application is ported using OpenACC. The developed method obtained a high performance of 64.4% of the FP64 peak, and obtained a 2.54-fold speedup from a conventional equation-based solver. We also showed that 85% to 93% of the performance obtained using the native programming environment CUDA can be obtained by the OpenACC implementations. In this way, it was shown that by constructing an appropriate algorithm, high performance can be achieved on GPUs even when using a low implementation cost programming method such as OpenACC. The approach presented in this paper is considered to be effective in other directive-based programming models, and is expected to contribute to low-cost development of high-performance HPC applications combining data-driven and equation-based methods currently under development in various fields.

Acknowledgments. Results were obtained using AI Bridging Cloud Infrastructure (ABCI) at National Institute of Advanced Industrial Science and Technology (AIST). This work was supported by MEXT as "Program for Promoting Researches on the Supercomputer Fugaku" (Large-scale numerical simulation of earthquake generation, wave propagation and soil amplification: hp200126, hp210171) and JSPS KAKENHI Grant Numbers JP18H05239, JP18H03795, JP17K14719.

References

1. ABCI System Overview. AIST. https://docs.abci.ai/en/system-overview/. Accessed 08 Oct 2021
2. About Fugaku. https://www.r-ccs.riken.jp/en/fugaku/about/. Accessed 24 Aug 2021
3. AI Bridging Cloud Infrastructure (ABCI): National Institute of Advanced Industrial Science and Technology (AIST). https://abci.ai/en/about_abci/. Accessed 08 Oct 2021
4. Chainer. https://chainer.org/. Accessed 24 Aug 2021
5. NVIDIA A100 TENSOR CORE GPU. https://www.nvidia.com/en-us/data-center/a100/. Accessed 24 Aug 2021
6. NVIDIA GPUDirect. https://developer.nvidia.com/gpudirect. Accessed 24 Aug 2021
7. NVIDIA V100 TENSOR CORE GPU. https://www.nvidia.com/en-us/data-center/a100/. Accessed 24 Aug 2021
8. OpenACC. http://www.openacc.org/. Accessed 24 Aug 2021
9. Arayeshnia, A., Keshtkar, A., Amiri, S.: Realistic human head voxel model for brain microwave imaging. In: 2017 Iranian Conference on Electrical Engineering (ICEE), pp. 1660–1663. IEEE (2017). https://doi.org/10.1109/iraniancee.2017.7985315

10. Chuang, P.-Y., Foertter, F.S.: An example of porting PETSc applications to heterogeneous platforms with OpenACC. In: Chandrasekaran, S., Juckeland, G. (eds.) WACCPD 2017. LNCS, vol. 10732, pp. 3–19. Springer, Cham (2018). https://doi.org/10.1007/978-3-319-74896-2_1
11. Golub, G.H., Ye, Q.: Inexact preconditioned conjugate gradient method with inner-outer iteration. SIAM J. Sci. Comput. **21**, 1305–1320 (1999)
12. Gotz, M., Anzt, H.: Machine learning-aided numerical linear algebra: convolutional neural networks for the efficient preconditioner generation. In: 2018 IEEE/ACM 9th Workshop on Latest Advances in Scalable Algorithms for Large-Scale Systems (ScalA), pp. 49–56. IEEE (2018). https://doi.org/10.1109/scala.2018.00010
13. Ichimura, T., Fujita, K., Hori, M., Maddegedara, L., Ueda, N., Kikuchi, Y.: A fast scalable iterative implicit solver with green's function-based neural networks. In: 2020 IEEE/ACM 11th Workshop on Latest Advances in Scalable Algorithms for Large-Scale Systems (ScalA), pp. 61–68. IEEE (2020). https://doi.org/10.1109/scala51936.2020.00013
14. Liang, J., Hua, R., Zhang, H., Zhu, W., Fu, Y.: Accelerated molecular dynamics simulation of Silicon Crystals on TaihuLight using OpenACC. Parallel Comput. **99**, 102667 (2020). https://doi.org/10.1016/j.parco.2020.102667
15. Londhe, A., et al.: Adaptively accelerating FWM2DA seismic modelling program on multi-core CPU and GPU architectures. Comput. Geosci. **146**, 104637 (2021). https://doi.org/10.1016/j.cageo.2020.104637
16. Sappl, J., Seiler, L., Harders, M., Rauch, W.: Deep learning of preconditioners for conjugate gradient solvers in urban water related problems (2019)
17. Shan, H., Zhao, Z., Wagner, M.: Accelerating the performance of modal aerosol module of E3SM using OpenACC. In: Wienke, S., Bhalachandra, S. (eds.) WACCPD 2019. LNCS, vol. 12017, pp. 47–65. Springer, Cham (2020). https://doi.org/10.1007/978-3-030-49943-3_3
18. Winget, J.M., Hughes, T.J.: Solution algorithms for nonlinear transient heat conduction analysis employing element-by-element iterative strategies. Comput. Methods Appl. Mech. Eng. **52**(1), 711–815 (1985). https://doi.org/10.1016/0045-7825(85)90015-5
19. Xue, W., Roy, C.J.: Multi-GPU performance optimization of a computational fluid dynamics code using OpenACC. Concurr. Comput. Pract. Exp. **33**(5), e6036 (2020). https://doi.org/10.1002/cpe.6036
20. Yamaguchi, T., et al.: GPU implementation of a sophisticated implicit low-order finite element solver with FP21-32-64 computation using OpenACC. In: Wienke, S., Bhalachandra, S. (eds.) WACCPD 2019. LNCS, vol. 12017, pp. 3–24. Springer, Cham (2020). https://doi.org/10.1007/978-3-030-49943-3_1

Challenges Porting a C++ Template-Metaprogramming Abstraction Layer to Directive-Based Offloading

Jeffrey Kelling[1]([✉])[ID], Sergei Bastrakov[2][ID], Alexander Debus[2][ID],
Thomas Kluge[2][ID], Matt Leinhauser[3,4][ID], Richard Pausch[2][ID],
Klaus Steiniger[2][ID], Jan Stephan[4][ID], René Widera[2][ID], Jeff Young[4,5][ID],
Michael Bussmann[4][ID], Sunita Chandrasekaran[3][ID], and Guido Juckeland[1][ID]

[1] Department of Information Services and Computing,
Helmholtz-Zentrum Dresden-Rossendorf (HZDR), Bautzner Landstr. 400,
01328 Dresden, Germany
j.kelling@hzdr.de
[2] Insitute of Radiation Physics, Helmholtz-Zentrum Dresden-Rossendorf (HZDR),
Bautzner Landstr. 400, 01328 Dresden, Germany
[3] Department of CIS, University of Delaware, Newark, DE 19716, USA
[4] Center for Advance Systems Understanding (CASUS), Am Untermarkt 20,
02826 Görlitz, Germany
[5] Georgia Tech, School of Computer Science, Atlanta, GA 30332, USA

Abstract. HPC systems employ a growing variety of compute accelerators with different architectures and from different vendors. Large scientific applications are required to run efficiently across these systems but need to retain a single code-base in order to not stifle development. Directive-based offloading programming models set out to provide the required portability, but, to existing codes, they themselves represent yet another API to port to. Here, we present our approach of porting the GPU-accelerated particle-in-cell code PIConGPU to OpenACC and OpenMP target by adding two new backends to its existing C++-template metaprogramming-based offloading abstraction layer alpaka and avoiding other modifications to the application code. We introduce our approach in the face of conflicts between requirements and available features in the standards as well as practical hurdles posed by immature compiler support.

Keywords: C++ · OpenACC · OpenMP · Offloading

1 Introduction

Contemporary scientific applications are often written with accelerators, like GPUs, in mind. This approach is required to make use of many modern compute clusters and supercomputers, but it brings a dilemma of choice from a zoo of proprietary and open offloading APIs coming with varying degrees of support form hardware vendors. While vendor specific, proprietary APIs usually

© Springer Nature Switzerland AG 2022
S. Bhalachandra et al. (Eds.): WACCPD 2021, LNCS 13194, pp. 92–111, 2022.
https://doi.org/10.1007/978-3-030-97759-7_5

promise best performance and hardware support, their use limits an application to one vendor's ecosystem. Open APIs offer portability, but cannot guarantee support on future hardware. Committing to any particular offloading API may thus necessitate future rewrites of software when new hardware or architectures become available or the chosen API looses support, which may be unfeasible with the limited time-budged for software development available within the scientific community. Porting even between similar offloading APIs has in the past also proven to be a non-trivial task [22].

With C++ being very prevalent in contemporary HPC, one approach to mitigate this problem of choice is to use this language's strength in zero-overhead abstraction via templates and template metaprogramming (TMP) to create an abstraction layer which applications can use to formulate parallelism in an API agnostic way. At first glance this only moves the support problem from the offloading API to the abstraction layer, however, in relation to a large scientific application such an abstraction layer is much smaller and thus requires much less work to port to new parallel APIs. Thus, such an abstraction layer is first conceived as a part of one or a group of scientific applications rather than a library for a general audience. Despite this focus, it will lend itself to other applications, with support being guaranteed as long as the primary applications fuel its developer's interest.

Another breed of open-standard APIs for parallelization and offloading are directive-based approaches which try to minimize changes to an existing, sequential code base by employing directives for marking code regions which may be offloaded by the compiler without modifying the code in it base-language to the eyes of a compiler with support not enabled. Like with any other API, their practical portability depends on the development afforded by compiler and hardware vendors, too. Currently two competing directive-based model that target accelerator offloading are being developed: OpenMP [12], which has be around since 1997 as a parallel model for multi-core CPUs, has been extended with `target` directives in version 4.0 of its standard, while OpenACC [8] was initially created to provide offloading to accelerators exclusively.

This paper presents our efforts and experiences in porting the computational radiation physics code PIConGPU [18] to both OpenACC and OpenMP `target`. PIConGPU uses alpaka [25], which was first developed to provide portable between different accelerator architectures, including GPUs and Intel MIC, as well as multi-core CPUs to PIConGPU. Even though the primary purpose of OpenMP and OpenACC is to simplify porting of existing codes, porting a code like PIConGPU, with alpaka, as a C++ abstraction layer, already in place, the code for two new alpaka back-ends requires much less effort than porting the whole of PIConGPU directly. Thus, the majority of this paper is dedicated to documenting our efforts to create alpaka back-ends for both OpenACC and OpenMP `target`. Some of the lessons learned here will also apply to using directives in C++ codes in general and specifically other C++ offloading abstraction layers.

PIConGPU is an extremely scalable, heterogeneous, fully relativistic particlein-cell (PIC) C++ code. This code has been chosen as one of the eight CAAR codes across the United States by the Oak Ridge National Laboratory. CAAR stands for Center for Acceleration Application Readiness - a program at ORNL that is created to ready applications for their next generation computing system, Frontier, the first exascale system to be in place later this year, 2021. Work in this paper narrates challenges and potential solutions to prepare such large scale applications for the ever changing hardware platforms.

This paper discusses the aspects of programmability, portability and performance via the following contributions:

- challenges porting PIConGPU to a directive-based programming model,
- creating alpaka back-ends for OpenMP and OpenACC and evaluating the functionalities of the available compilers, and
- highlighting compiler and runtime issues throughout the PIConGPU code migration process.

We provide an overview of various offloading APIs and abstraction libraries in Sect. 2. In Sect. 3 the employed APIs and alpaka are reviewed and compared. During the porting process, various issues with both standards and compiler support were encountered which are described in Sect. 4. In Sect. 5 we first discuss the major obstacles we faced during this effort, then provide a short overview of which examples already work using our OpenMP target and OpenACC alpaka backends and current compilers. Finally, Sect. 6 concludes with an outlook on the developments in the OpenMP and OpenACC ecosystems.

2   Related Work

Since the dawn of general purpose computing on GPUs (GPGPU), quite a few offloading APIs have come and gone. One notable open, cross vendor entry is the Khronos Group's OpenCL [9] which is barely used anymore in HPC mostly due veining vendor support in this space and partly due to its choice of having device code separate from the host source. Other APIs use a *single-source* approach, where offloaded code is integrated into the host language. NVIDIA's proprietary compute unified device architecture (CUDA) [4], which is older than the OpenCL standard, is a C/C++ dialect which offers single-source offloading. It is the most widely used API for scientific codes today, having evolved into the go-to API for many scientific application developers. In response to CUDA's popularity, AMD created Heterogeneous-compute Interface for Portability (HIP), which mimics the CUDA API to simplify porting CUDA codes. Later single-source approaches aimed at integrating offloading into standard C++ without creating a dialect. This was first attempted by Microsoft introducing C++ AMP [3], which inspired Khronos' SYCL [15]. The `do concurrent` construct introduced to Fortran in version 2008, which can also be offloaded to GPUs by some compilers [24], is a more mature example of the drive to include offloading support directly into base languages.

With these and more offloading APIs, including OpenMP `target` and Open-ACC, available to chose from obsolescence is always looming and can not only be caused by a vendor dropping support for an API, but also by technical developments: With the prevalence NVIDIA GPUs in supercomputers, CUDA looked like a safe choice not long ago. A switch to an AMD-based machine could be addressed by an, in theory, not too demanding port to HIP. However, both of these APIs can only target GPUs not the host CPUs which are the primary compute resource installed on the currently fastest supercomputer Fugaku [17], meaning a code based on these APIs would not be able to run in such a system. Therefore, C++ abstraction layers do not only aim to be a bridge between accelerator architectures and APIs, but also include sequential and parallel execution on the host.

Sandia National Laboratories started the development of Kokkos [21] to achieve performance portability for scientific codes written in C++. It currently supports CUDA, OpenMP (host), native POSIX threads and HPX. Another library is RAJA [13], developed at Lawrence Livermore National Laboratory, which offers support of CUDA, HIP, Thread Building Blocks (TBB) and OpenMP (including `target`). RAJA also specifically aims to provide parallel algorithms like Thrust [16]. These libraries, just like alpaka, are single-source, passing user code as a predicate to templates which encapsulate the underlying back-end APIs. In contrast to these examples, alpaka aims to be lightweight low-level abstraction, providing generic access to the basic parallel hierarchies of accelerators without shaping user code prescribing memory layout or algorithms [23].

Another approach that should be mentioned is that of a template expression library, where user code is not directly passed to a back-end but written in TMP-based domain specific language which then generates backend-compatible code. VexCL [10] used this approach to generate code for just-in-time compilation (JIT) to support OpenCL, next to CUDA and OpenMP.

3   Methods and APIs

3.1   Alpaka and PIConGPU

PIConGPU is a plasma physics code that simulates the dynamics of fast charged particles in electromagnetic fields taking into account relativistic effects and fields generated by moving particles. The employed particle-in-cell approach does store electric and magnetic fields on a regular grid but also must keep track of quickly moving particles. Particles are stored on a per-supercell basis using a dynamic collection of fixed-sized particle vectors. Kernels implementing particle-grid operations on GPUs collectively copy nearby field values between device memory and on-chip scratch memory (e.g. `_shared_` in CUDA) to facilitate efficient parallel processing of particles. This approach takes the hierarchical architecture of GPUs into account and was initially implemented using CUDA directly.

PIConGPU uses templates and TMP to provide a domain-specific language (DSL) for the user to describe the types of particles, interactions and external fields present in the simulation. Some numerical parameters of these are also fixed at compile time. This incurs a large number of `constexpr` variables of static lifetime, either as static class members or global inside namespaces, to be defined as part of the simulation definition.

Alpaka was introduced to make PIConGPU portable without duplicating code for different target architectures while retaining the present performance on GPUs. To this end, alpaka provides abstract forms of all major concepts present in CUDA, including the execution hierarchy, atomics, block-level synchronization primitives and shared memory as well as a generalize device and memory management API. To generalize these concepts alpaka provides a rather verbose API. To simplify porting codes from CUDA to alpaka the wrapper library cupla [5] was created which provides a simplified API which is more similar to CUDA. Other applications also adopted alpaka as their abstraction for offloading, such as a ptychography code and a high-level trigger software in a large-scale particle detector.

Alpaka currently provides a backend targeting sequential execution, backends for parallel execution on the host via OpenMP and TBB, as well as on GPUs using CUDA and HIP. A SYCL backend is also under development [2]. Alpaka's codebase [1] contains some examples, ranging from a parallel "Hello World" to Euler integration. All backends are also covered by a suite of tests, each of which tests a different aspect of offloading. One test focuses on transferring memory between buffers on host and device, including multiple cases covering different source and device locations and buffer sizes. Other tests cover aspects of kernel execution on the device, like trivial kernels, variables in block-shared memory, synchronization between threads or atomic operations.

3.2   Review of OpenACC and OpenMP Target

Both OpenACC and OpenMP `target` have been designed with GPUs or similar accelerators as offload target devices in mind. Both expose the same two main layers of parallelization on target devices as known from GPUs: A work grid is first decomposed into loosely coupled blocks executing independently, which in turn decompose into threads which execute in at least such a way that data sharing may be exclusively between threads of the same block. Both models can also target CPUs, where implementations tend to limit the number of threads per block, often to one, in order to effectively map blocks to CPU threads. An overview on the names the different models assign to these layers is provided in Table 1. We will stick to the CUDA/Alpaka naming scheme.

OpenACC adds a third innermost layer called `vector` as a straight continuation of this concept, which could conceivably be translated in the same way as OpenMP's `simd` loop on some architectures. While alpaka does provide an `element` layer inside threads, no abstraction is provided beyond offering a work-partitioning concept to support canonical `for` loops, ideally with compile-time

Table 1. Rosetta-stone for the names of parallel execution layers. The `element/simd` layer is only listed for completeness. Each model using a different set of terms pollutes the name space, which is why we stick to the CUDA/Alpaka terminology in the text. Where the word "worker" is used it refers to a scheduled unit executing some work on any parallel level, not to the OpenACC `worker`.

CUDA	Alpaka	OpenMP 5.0	OpenACC 3.0
grid	grid	(target)	(parallel)
block	block	team	gang
thread	thread	thread	worker
—	element	simd	(vector)

length which a compiler can automatically vectorize.[1] As this layer is not going to be mapped explicitly we are not covering it further.

Both models provide directives to control parallel execution and data movement between host and device. Directives start with

> `#pragma acc ...`   in OpenACC and
>
> `#pragma omp ...`   in OpenMP.

Here, we shall briefly review the basic primitives of the OpenACC 3.0 [7] and OpenMP 5.0 [10] APIs to highlight their primary design aspects that affect our porting efforts.

Execution of code on the device is initiated using the directives `acc parallel` and `omp target`. OpenMP provides the directives `teams` and `parallel` which cause regions of code to be executed by multiple blocks or threads, but do not imply any distribution of work. Loops can be distributed in these regions using the `distribute` (blocks) and `for` (threads) directives. In OpenACC parallel execution and work distribution constructs are inseparably linked with work distribution provided by the `loop gang` and `loop worker` constructs. Herein lies the main conceptual difference between the OpenMP and OpenACC programming models: While OpenMP aims to support all types of parallelism, OpenACC is exclusively designed to describe data parallelism in device code.

On GPUs no assumptions about the execution order of blocks should be made, which is reflected in OpenMP not allowing synchronization and locks across blocks, it does, however, support them between threads of the same block, using `barrier` and `critical`, respectively. Following its exclusively data-parallel paradigm, OpenACC does not make any assumptions on execution order on any level and thus does not support explicit synchronization and locks. Because a `loop gang` region may contain multiple loops in sequence marked with `loop worker` and `loop vector` synchronization can be achieved implicitly within blocks.

---

[1] Alpaka is following the approach of very long instruction word (VLIW) architectures in OpenCL in this aspect.

Table 2. Overview of OpenMP and OpenACC manual memory management routines with CUDA versions listed as reference.

CUDA	OpenMP 5.0	OpenACC 3.0
cudaMalloc	omp_target_alloc	acc_malloc
cudaMemcpy	omp_target_memcpy	acc_memcpy_to_device
		acc_memcpy_from_device
		acc_memcpy_device
cudaFree	omp_target_free	acc_free

Both APIs support atomic operations through an `atomic` directive. OpenMP defines atomics as binding to the target device, OpenACC is less clear on this aspect, only stating that operations are atomic between gangs.

OpenMP provides the runtime API functions `omp_get_team_num()` to determine the id of a block in device code and `omp_get_thread_num()` determine the id of a thread within a block. OpenACC does not provide this functionality because in its strict map-reduce picture only the work items must be identified, the workers may remain anonymous to the application code.

Data Management and Declarations. The canonical way of moving data between host and device in these models is by declaring host storage locations to be associated to locations in device memory and later, or in the same construct, instructing the runtime to copy data between the host and associated device locations. We will not elaborate on the `omp target data` and `acc data` directives because in our port we are using runtime API functions which allow for explicit memory management instead. These are listed in Table 2.

Clauses related to data movement may also be present in `omp target` and `acc parallel` constructs where they declare how the listed variables should be handled before the start and after the end of the attached region. On the Open-ACC side these include `copy`, `copyin`, `copyout`, `create` and others. OpenMP uses the `map` clause, which handles details through a `map-type` attribute.

Global variables, including compile-time constants, must be *declared* for presence on the device. In OpenACC this is done through the construct `acc declare copyin( varList )`, where *varList* is a list variables that are declared for the device. With OpenMP global variables can be made available to device code either, in a similar way, using the `omp declare target( varList )` construct or by declaring them inside a `declare target` region. Implementations relax this requirement and only require declaration of compile time constants if they are not optimized out and the compiler places the value in run-time memory. Violations of this relaxed requirement get expressed as linker errors.

Similar constructs are also used to declare functions to be compiled for the device, so they can be called from offloaded code in other compilation units.

Functions defined in the same compilation unit can be called without having been declared for the device.

3.3   Experimental Setup

Initially, we started out testing various compilers. For the OpenMP we tried *Clang*, AMD's Clang-based development compiler AOMP version 0.7, AMD's ROC variant of Clang version 4.3.0 (based on Clang 13) [14], GCC version 9, and IBM XL version 16.1.1-5. For OpenACC NVIDIA's *NVHPC* toolkit versions from 20.3 to 21.7 and GCC versions 9 through 11 were used. We stopped testing with GCC and IBM XL due to fixes to reported bugs not becoming available timely enough to fit the scope of this work. In the case of IBM XL, debugging runtime errors also turned out to be infeasible due to prohibitively long compile times. We dropped AOMP due repeated difficulty building new releases and also most fixes to bugs AOMP inherited from upstream clang being available upstream first.

Extensive testing was done only for OpenMP using Clang version 10 and above, primarily tracking the `main` branch, targeting host ($\times 86^2$) and AMD GPUs (HSA[3]) and for OpenACC using the latest NVHPC release, currently 21.7, targeting host ($\times 86$ see Footnote 2) and NVIDIA GPUs[4]. We only used ROC Clang for a few tests prior to this paper. Our testing was strictly focussed on functionality and therefore performance was not measured.

4   Porting Alpaka

With PIConGPU using alpaka to abstract parallel execution models, the only viable way of porting it to OpenMP and OpenACC is to create two alpaka backends and, ideally, not touch PIConGPU itself at all. This severely reduces the amount of code required for the port because each alpaka feature only needs to be mapped to the respective target model once, resulting in most relevant OpenMP and OpenACC construct being used only once in the code.

Alpaka breaks down any offloading backend into a set of basic concepts which are separately implemented and tied together. Table 3 lists the most relevant of these.

Executing User Code on Device. For each backend, alpaka provides a type `TaskKernelBackendName` which wraps a user-provided functor containing the payload code as well as the arguments that should be passed to the functor on-device for execution in a `Queue`. This is where alpaka's parallel levels get mapped onto the levels provided by the backend. The listing in Fig. 1 illustrates

---

[2] Intel i7-4930K, Ubuntu 18.04.
[3] Radeon Vega 64, Ubuntu 18.04.
[4] GTX Titan Black, Ubuntu 18.04.

```
1   template<class Functor, class... Args>
2   void TaskKernel_OpenMP5_OpenACC (
3     WorkDiv workDiv,    // grid size
4     Functor functor,    // user functor
5     Args ... args )     // user arguments
6   {
7
8     // OpenMP
9   # pragma omp target
10    {
11  # pragma omp teams distribute
12      for ( int blockIdx = 0;
13        blockIdx < workDiv.blocks;
14        ++blockIdx )
15      {
16        AccOmp5 ctx ( workDiv, blockIdx ); // OpenMP backend handle
17  #       pragma omp parallel
18        {
19          functor ( ctx, args... );
20        }
21      }
22    }
23
24    // OpenACC
25  # pragma acc parallel
26    {
27  #     pragma acc loop gang
28      for ( int blockIdx = 0;
29        blockIdx < workDiv.blocks;
30        ++blockIdx )
31      {
32        CtxBlockOacc ctxBlock ( workDiv, blockIdx ); // OpenACC backend handle
33  #       pragma acc loop worker
34        for ( int threadIdx = 0;
35          threadIdx < workDiv.threads;
36          ++threadIdx )
37        {
38          // need to add threadIdx to the context info
39          AccOacc ctx ( ctxBlock, threadIdx );
40          functor ( ctx, args... );
41        }
42      }
43    }
44  }
```

Fig. 1. Sketch of the structure of a `TaskKernel` template which calls a user-provided functor with user-provided argument in a parallel context using OpenMP or OpenACC, also providing a handle `ctx` to enable the user to generically access abstracted backend features. Note, that in the actual implementation `TaskKernel` is a class template which stores the functor and the arguments as members and provides a call operator to provide the functionality sketched above.

Table 3. List of selected primary concepts which need to be implemented by any alpaka backend.

`Acc`	A type that acts as a handle for a backend. It can be used at compile time to select implementations of traits related to the backend and thus ties all parts of a backend together.
`AtomicGrids` `AtomicBlocks` `AtomicThreads`	Atomic operations which can be implemented differently for atomicity at each level of parallelization: on the whole target device, between block of a kernel, between threads of a block.
`BlockSharedDyn`	A block-shared memory buffer of a size that is set at run time.
`BlockSharedSt`	A strategy to declare block-shared variable akin to CUDA's `__shared__`.
`BlockSync`	A strategy by which to synchronize threads within a block.
`Buf`	A RAII class managing a memory buffer in a target device.
`Dev`	A handle for a target device.
`IdxBt`	A strategy by which a thread can determine its id within a block.
`IdxGb`	A strategy by which a block can determine its id within a kernel.
`Queue`	A type that implements an execution queue on a target device.
`TaskKernel`	A class that wraps user code for execution on a target device.
`WorkDiv`	A type holding information about the requested sizes of the grid, blocks and threads (number of elements) for kernel execution.

the basic structure of what the alpaka `TaskKernel` invocation could look like for both OpenMP and OpenACC.

A block-shared variable `ctx` is declared inside the `teams`, respectively `loop gang`, region, but outside of the `omp parallel`, respectively `loop worker` region, to represent a block-context handle to the thread. This context information includes the current block id. More details about this are provided in the following.

Memory. Alpaka's implementation adheres to the resource acquisition is initialization (RAII) principle and provides a buffer type for memory on each device, including the host. Therefore, alpaka does not have a concept of fixed associations between host and device memory, but rather allows copying data between (sections of) any pair of buffers. One implication of this is, that the buffer types for OpenMP and OpenACC must be implemented using the manual management routines listed in Table 2, but more importantly, that any pointer to data used in device code, will be a device pointer with no associated host memory. This leads to different complications with each of the models.

By default both models map local variables, including function parameters to the device automatically if they are required in the device code. OpenMP assumes that any pointer it maps hence contains a host address and tries to replace it by the associated device address. If no associated address exists the value copied to the device is 0x0, which also applies to original device point-ers. The OpenMP runtime can be instructed to copy a device pointer verbatim using the is_device_ptr(*varName*) clause on the target directive in line 9 or on additional omp target data directives, which alpaka cannot use directly because any pointers are elements of a parameter pack and thus have no name. OpenMP will not perform this replacement on pointers which are enclosed in other data types. Thus, we can get around this problem by wrapping any kernel parameters, which are provided by the user in a C++ parameter pack, in an std::tuple or similar structure.

OpenACC performs a similar replacement of address values also for pointers found inside structures which are mapped, taking the wrapping-workaround off the table. Like in OpenMP, a variable can be explicitly declared as a device pointer using the deviceptr(*varName*) clause on the parallel directive in line 25, which is not possible because there is no way to know which parameters contain pointers without access to static reflection. The only other option is to add the clause default(present) telling the runtime to assume, that all variables referenced in the offloaded code are already present on the device and do not need to be mapped. Unfortunately this also disables automatic mapping of local variables, necessitating that all local host variables used in the parallel region occur in a copyin clause, which is feasible because they are named.

Block and Thread Index. Each worker needs access to information about its position in the global execution grid in order for work distribution to work. The OpenACC variant below line 25 does basically show the canonical way of distributing work over blocks and threads verbatim. In alpaka, the indices of these two nested loops are passed to the user code in ctx. Because OpenMP provides a build-in way to retrieve the thread index via omp_get_thread_num() we use a parallel region without loop to avoid the overhead passing another loop counter to the user code, while the compiler may use hardware intrinsics to supply the user code with this information.

Atomic Operations. The set of atomic operations supported by alpaka fol-lows the set provided by CUDA. This includes operations like atomic compare and swap (CAS), min and max next to binary operations. Both OpenMP and OpenACC support atomic load and store as well as binary operations with both a pure update and a capture semantic, i.e. atomically retrieving the stored value before applying the operation to the memory location. Only OpenMP 5.1 adds an atomic compare clause [11], which permits the ternary operator which is required to implement CAS, min and max.

As a work-around these ternary operations can be implemented using a critical region, which, however, does not exist in OpenACC. Not supporting these operations is not an option as PIConGPU's on-device dynamic memory allocator mallocMC [6] requires them. Therefore we had to implement critical region in violation of the OpenACC standard using device-global, grid-level and block-level locks based on more basic atomics to cover all levels at which atomic operations may be required.

Block-Shared Memory. Alpaka provides block-shared variables in the same way CUDA does, i.e. declaration of them is allowed at any point inside kernel/thread code. This is not supported by our targeted models. This capability is implemented by providing a block-shared small-object allocator `BlockSharedSt` as part of the `ctx` object, which contains a fixed-size member array as underlying buffer. The size of this array can only be set at compile time. Allocations of such shared variables are carried out by a master thread, requiring synchronization between threads of a block, after which a reference to the allocated memory is returned to all threads. A part of aforementioned buffer can be reserved as a shared buffer of run time-size (`BlockSharedDyn`), analogous to CUDA dynamic shared memory.

Our expectation is, that implementations will in time be optimized to actually store block-shared variables which fit into on-chip memory there when targeting GPUs. As long as these variables are stored in global device memory our strategy will at least allow these variables to reside compactly in a cache close to executing block.

OpenMP 5.0 added the `omp allocate` directive which allows explicit allocation of memory through the OpenMP runtime, including an implementation-defined allocator `omp_pteam_mem_alloc` which may allow the declaration of block-shared memory akin to using CUDA's `_shared_` attribute. We did not test this option yet, because functionally, albeit conceivably with lower performance, we can make due with the implementation described above, which is required for OpenACC either way, and using this feature could open another angle where incomplete OpenMP 5.0 compiler support may hit us.

Block-Level Barrier. Alpaka provides a block-level barrier akin to CUDA's `__syncthreads()` which can be implemented in OpenMP using the `omp barrier` directive.

OpenACC does not support any explicit synchronization, so we again violated the OpenACC standard by implementing a barrier using atomic operations and spin loops on counters stored in the block-shared context variable `ctx`. This implementation works on GPUs in practice as long as the OpenACC runtime executes exactly the number of threads per block the code expects it to.

4.1   Final Touches: PIConGPU

PIConGPU uses one global variable on the target device which is not abstracted by alpaka and thus must be declared by an `acc declare device_resident(` *varName* `)`, respectively `omp declare target(` *varName* `)`, directive in the PIConGPU code.

Global `constexpr` variables, used primarily as part of the simulation definition, for the most part only exist at compile time and influence what code is generated for offloading. Constants whose value the compiler cannot optimize out do require explicit mapping to the device. This is the case for arrays which are dynamically indexed at run time and any other constant the address of which taken in any context, e.g. if it is used as `this` argument of a member function call. We chose to not map constants without run time storage explicitly to limit our changes to the application code outside of alpaka to a minimum.

5 Major Hurdles and Discussion

5.1 Standards Issues

OpenACC/OpenMP: Static `constexpr` Mapping. Both OpenACC and OpenMP require global variables to be marked explicitly for availability in device code, making no exception for compile-time constants, so formally all compile time constants have to be declared for the target.[5] In a code like PIConGPU this would effectively lead to each simulation definition file starting with `omp declare target` and ending with `omp end declare target` or, worse, `acc declare copyin( listOfAllConstexpr )`. While the OpenMP version of this only makes the declare construct devoid of meaning, the OpenACC version actually hurts the code maintainability because each addition or removal of a constant has to be mirrored in a second place.

Most available implementations only raise warnings when a `constexpr` variable is referenced in a target region without having been mapped because there is no problem unless the compiler determines, that a `constexpr` must be addressed at run time. In this case a reference to a symbol is generated, but no definition, eventually leading to errors during dynamic linking at run time.

For compile time constants, the standards should require symbols to be generated for `constexpr` variables that are defined inline if needed, as it is easier for the compiler to determine if a given `constexpr` require a run time representation then for the programmer. This would be more consistent with inline functions, or functions defined within the same translation unit in general, not requiring a `declare` to be callable from an offloaded region. It would also better fit the C++-notion, that the compiler decides how to handle `constexpr`.

OpenMP: static `constexpr` Members. We started this work with only OpenMP 4.5 being supported by compilers which required types to not contain any `static` data members for them to be considered mappable to target, with no exception for compile time constants. Most compilers would only warn if mapped types contained `static` compile time constants. However, GCC did throw an error here, which prevented us from performing any testing of GCC's OpenMP or OpenACC[6] implementations with PIConGPU where, as in any TMP code, `static constexpr` data members are too commonplace to be removed as a workaround. OpenMP 5.0 solves this problem by removing the restriction on `static` data members altogether.

---

[5] In [10]: Sect. 2.10.4, Restrictions, bullet 5.
[6] OpenACC does not actually have this restriction, but GCC's implementation is based on the OpenMP implementation and thus inherited this check.

OpenACC: Lack of Explicit Block-Level Synchronization. The lack of an explicit block-level thread barrier is the most prominent issue our OpenACC port faces in terms of production-readiness. Although we do have a functioning workaround for it, based on the standard not allowing any assumption on thread scheduling, it is correct in stating, that our solution using atomics and spin loops is not save. In practice this issue is exacerbated by the standard API not providing any way to ascertain the actual number of threads being run per block nor to force a certain number to be run, leaving it to the user to find the maximum number of threads the runtime will actually run per block on a given platform and instruct alpaka to not request more than this. If the number actually running threads is smaller than expected, our barrier implementation will dead-lock.

Any need for synchronization between threads could in theory be served using only the implicit barrier after a `loop worker` region, but this is not feasible in practice. On the surface this would require changing all kernels in PIConGPU which employ barriers to employ loops to describe block-level parallelism, circumventing the existing abstractions and introducing a second implementation incompatible with, e.g., the CUDA backend. Even deeper structural changes would be required where PIConGPU uses other libraries based on alpaka: MallocMC provides an alpaka device function which returns information about the allocator to all threads of a block using collective operations which require synchronization inside the function.

When targeting any hardware which does actually not allow any assumptions about threat execution but somehow still supports the implicit barrier after a `loop worker` region, a compiler could still implement an explicit barrier by first inlining the code surrounding the barrier and then reordering it to split it into one region before the barrier and one after. Some transformations required to achieve this may require assertions about the code to be made which the base language does not allow in general, e.g. swapping of inner and outer loops. Considering, that any code where data dependencies block the required transformations would be using the barrier in an invalid way, often leading to a dead-lock at run time, the compiler could raise an error when it fails to transform the code to make the barrier implicit.

C++: `std:tuple` Trivial Copy. When it comes to offloading, it is very important, that types can be copied bit-wise in order to transfer instances to the target. The C++ standard template library (STL) defines the type trait `std::is_trivially_copyable` which, if true, guarantees that a bit-wise copy is safe for the given type. Composite types of trivially copyable types are trivially copyable if the move and copy constructors and assignment operators are trivial. For any type which is mapped to target, clang checks this condition and issues a warning when it is not met.

The C++ STL provides the type `std::tuple` which is very useful, among other things, when storing parameter packs for later use, or to sneak device pointers past the address mapping of the OpenMP runtime. Unfortunately, the C++ standard does not require implementations of `std::tuple` to be trivially copyable if all component types are. Both the GNU libstdc++ and LLVM's libc++ implement `std::tuple` in a way that removes the `std::is_trivially_copyable` trait. While they can still be copied bit-wise in practice as long as all component types can be, this makes `std::tuple` effectively unusable for offloading, because its use turns an otherwise useful warning into noise. An active defect report against the C++ standard on this issue exists [20].

5.2   Compiler and Runtime Issues

PIConGPU is a rather large application, combing through almost all of the C++ core language and, while alpaka only requires a subset of OpenMP or OpenACC to implement its API, it probably happens to lean on aspects which are usually not a focus when porting legacy applications, such as a wide range of atomic operations, data sharing at block level and manual memory management. Hence, the main roadblock to this work was, and remains, an immaturity of the compilers around OpenMP `target` and OpenACC as the specifications are rather new. Previously ported applications may use a common set of patterns, predominantly straight parallel unrolling of loops over arrays, which is what current compilers support best. When straying off the trodden path we find a number of compiler bugs. With respect to C++ features especially, existing test suites appear to contain mainly small examples each only using a very limited set.

The compiler/runtime bugs can be grouped roughly into three categories: First internal compiler errors (ICEs) triggered in the compilers by the occurrence of, usually, more complex C++ constructs, e.g. lambdas or parameter packs, occurring in or around target regions. The second are ICEs in the backend, where either intermediate representations from host and target appear to get mixed up or plain missing features, like missing code generation for some atomics. If a code gets past these two, there are run time errors triggered by faulty code generation or runtime behavior.

The largest issue arising from all of these is that further development of triggering code is blocked until the compiler gets fixed; unless a simple work around is available, which turned out to be rare. Encountering a run time error is especially tricky, as, chances are, there is only one compiler successfully compiling an example for a specific target and thus there is no way to independently test whether the example code itself it correct.

Having only one large application, PIConGPU, that has to iterate with the compiler development and gets stuck at each encountered compiler bug would be too slow. In our work, we were able to take advantage of alpaka's example codes and test suite. With each small application only using a subset of the backend's features, some of which may trigger different errors first, we were able to report or debug those in parallel.

Close communication with compiler vendors also helps to alleviate the issue of code not being testable due a lack of reliable compilers. With the very fresh support of offloading, error messages raised by the compiler can often be misleading and fail to point at the actual issue. In some cases an ICE can be triggered by faulty user code, which is just handled badly inside the compiler. It is likely, that invalid code is not often part of compiler test suites.

ICEs are rather simple to report and caused either by incomplete implementations or some compiler internals which we cannot comment on. Run time errors caused by compiler bugs require debugging on our part. Issues we encountered that lead to wrong run time behavior of our program include an atomic capture which falsely did not change the addressed value and variables declared at block-level being shared between all blocks instead of being private to a single block. Bugs leading to the runtime actively raising an error are simpler to pin down, such as, e.g., a case where accessing an element of a struct member array which is above a certain size in bytes would cause the runtime to report a "GPU memory error".

Compiler Error Messages. Another problem encountered when debugging issues in C++ codes in general, specifically when using vendor compilers backed by smaller development teams, is unspecific error reporting. The minor part of this can be unspecific messages of the form "invalid something", which is almost useless information in the absence of a very verbose context description. The major problem is a lack of context information provided by non-mainstream compilers. There appears to be a strong focus on a procedural style of programming, leading to the assumption, that pointing to the line in the source code where an error occurs provides sufficient information—in C++ it does not: When a code instantiates a template, e.g., ten times, four of which contain something *invalid*, printing the same line number four times is not helpful. The fact, that g++ and clang++ compilers sometimes produce screens upon screens of a single error message in some template instantiation is a source of much ridicule of C++, but it is very important to have this information in any non-trivial application. Template instantiation generates code at compile time. Consequently, that one line may have four different meanings when the error occurs and six more different meanings where the template is instantiated without causing a compiler error. Thus, it is important for the programmer to know *which* instance of the template causes the error, otherwise they are left guessing.

We also observed bugs in the error reporting of compilers. For example, a compiler may print an error message pointing to the correct line number, but name the wrong file, specifically complaining about a line in a header, while giving the name of the main source file.

5.3   Preliminary Results

Despite complete alpaka backends for OpenMP target and OpenACC and explicit mappings of some bits of PIConGPU's code which circumvented the abstraction layer, PIConGPU still cannot be successfully ported to GPUs using OpenMP or OpenACC due to a number of open issues in compilers and runtimes as highlighted in the previous section. With Clang, we were able to use host as offload target for OpenMP. We had the same option with NVHPC and

OpenACC. We successfully ran PIConGPU via alpaka's OpenMP or OpenACC backend using recent versions of the respective compiler on the host.

HelloWorld is the most basic example for an alpaka application in that is only runs one kernel which does nothing but print the thread and block index of each thread. Successful execution shows, that the block-shared variables in Fig. 1, lines 16 or 32 could be created and that that they contain the correct block index for each block. This works on GPU with OpenACC using NVHPC. There is one major bit of complexity in this example though, in that it requires the runtime to provide `printf()` on target. Clang's offloading runtime for AMD GPUs does not provide this yet.

VectorAdd performs a simple addition of two vectors filled with random values on the device and checks the result on the host. This example includes copying data between host and device in both directions, next to executing a kernel containing a grid-strided loop. It is, however more portable than *helloWorld* in that is does not require any `c-lib` functions in offloaded code. This example works successfully on GPU both with OpenACC using NVHPC. With OpenMP targeting AMD GPUs this example works only with AMD's ROC Clang version 4.3.0, while with clang's `main` branch we see an issue where having large arrays as members in structs causes a memory error, which makes starting any alpaka kernel fail.

Alpaka Test Suite. Targeting the host, all tests pass with OpenMP and Open-ACC using clang 11+ and NVHPC 21.7, respectively.

Using the most current upstream clang[7], most tests compile targeting AMD GPUs, some fail with ICEs, two due to missing `cmath` symbols for device code. All tests fail at run time when using clang `main` because of the aforementioned issue crashing any alpaka kernel. Using ROC clang, the linker hangs with most of the tests.

With OpenACC, targeting NVIDIA GPUs, the majority of tests compile and succeed at run time. Most notably, tests of the block-level thread synchronization and block-shared memory succeed on GPU.

6   Conclusions and Outlook

This work attempted to map the feature set of the C++ template metaprogramming (TMP)-based accelerator abstraction layer alpaka to the directive-based APIs OpenMP `target` and OpenACC. The main conceptual difficulty is that alpaka's API set is heavily inspired by CUDA and thus requires some very specific capabilities to be implemented, such as the possibility for user code to declare block-shared variables anywhere instead of only up-front, which no existing API other than CUDA and it's look-alikes supports. Here, alpaka could

---

[7] Git commit c20cb5547ddd.

achieve better performance portability by relaxing its adherence to CUDA and instead providing a more general abstraction.

We described a number of problems with the present ecosystem encountered introducing directive-based models into a TMP-based and heavily abstracted C++ code, which any other abstraction layer, such as Kokkos of RAJA, aiming to support these models would have to face, too. These issues highlight, that the main for OpenMP and OpenACC use-case for these programming models is to add accelerator-offloading to legacy code, which are usually large Fortran or C code-bases. These programming languages mostly support a procedural programming paradigm and only offer a limited options for abstraction beyond this. C++ allows very high levels of abstraction using templates, which provides a quite rigorous formalism for code generation and meta-programming. This lack of consideration for C++ TMP makes the standards treat compile time constants like any other (global) variable. This seems reasonable in C or Fortran, where a compile time constant is little more than a variable that is known to the compiler to not change a runtime and that has a static life time. In C++, they can affect code generation itself, leading to the expectation, that handling them is the responsibility of the compiler. They may sometimes become a variable at runtime which does not change, but mostly their storage is optimized out. A distinction should be made between static life time and compile-time life time, where in the latter case the compiler should be responsible for mapping any data still needed at run time.

OpenACC aims to distinguish itself from OpenMP by offering a less explicit way describe parallelism in code. As in this work it was our goal map a very explicit model onto it, we could not appreciate this. From our perspective, the main distinction is OpenACC's strict adherence to data parallel principles. This is interesting from an academic perspective in that it might enforce a cleaner description of parallel code if fully embraced. When porting originally sequential code to OpenACC it may not be much of a problem to follow this path. We are, however, not aware of any hardware architecture in common use exhibiting the restrictions enforced by OpenACC. Likewise, no other offloading API enforces strict data parallelism, which causes existing parallel codes to be build around established features such as explicit barriers and accessible worker ids. Porting a code that relies on certain patterns to a programming model that does not offer them results in substantial changes to the code and may end up being more of a rewrite than a port, such as in the case of PIConGPU. In our view, this makes OpenACC not a viable general-purpose parallel programming model in its current form.

The primary issue we encountered was the immaturity of compilers both with respect to the support for OpenMP `target` and OpenACC as well the interaction of that support with C++ code. This forced us to follow a, nowadays, quite unusual development approach, were we had write our code without the possibility to validate it by compiling, because the compiler would fail at an internal compiler error (ICE). In order to progress we shifted our focus to compilers and targets where we saw the fastest development with respect to the issues we encountered. For this reason, we followed the clang mainline development on the OpenMP side. With OpenACC, we were only able to make significant progress due to active support from the NVHPC developers with finding and fixing bugs in their compiler and also testing our code with their development compilers in between releases.

We continue to follow the compiler development on both the OpenMP and OpenACC side to push towards improved compiler support and to address potential issues in the backends presented here.

Acknowledgments. We want to thank Mathew Colgrove (NVIDIA) and the NVHPC team for help with debugging both compiler and code issues, Ron Lieberman (AMD) for testing PIConGPU with AOMP and advice on Clang in general and the SPEC High Performance Group for testing and support. We acknowledge the IT Center of RWTH Aachen for access to their infrastructure and Jonas Hahnfeld for support.

This material is based upon work supported by the U.S. Department of Energy, Office of science, and this research used resources of the Oak Ridge Leadership Computing Facility at the Oak Ridge National Laboratory, which is supported by the Office of Science of the U.S. Department of Energy under Contract No. DE-AC05-00OR22725.

This work was partially funded by the Center of Advanced Systems Understanding (CASUS) which is financed by Germany's Federal Ministry of Education and Research (BMBF) and by the Saxon Ministry for Science, Culture and Tourism (SMWK) with tax funds on the basis of the budget approved by the Saxon State Parliament.

References

1. alpaka. https://github.com/alpaka-group/alpaka
2. Alpaka SYCL backend development. https://github.com/alpaka-group/alpaka/pull/789
3. C++ AMP. https://docs.microsoft.com/en-us/cpp/parallel/amp/cpp-amp-cpp-accelerated-massive-parallelism?view=msvc-160
4. CUDA. https://developer.nvidia.com/cuda-toolkit-archive
5. Cupla. https://github.com/alpaka-group/cupla
6. MallocMC. https://github.com/alpaka-group/mallocMC
7. OpenACC 3.0 API specification. https://www.openacc.org/sites/default/files/inline-images/Specification/OpenACC.3.0.pdf
8. OpenACC website. https://www.openacc.org
9. OpenCL. https://www.khronos.org/registry/OpenCL
10. OpenMP 5.0 API specification. https://www.openmp.org/spec-html/5.0/openmp.html
11. OpenMP 5.1 API specification – atomic. https://www.openmp.org/spec-html/5.1/openmpsu105.html
12. OpenMP website. https://www.openmp.org/
13. RAJA. https://github.com/LLNL/RAJA
14. ReadonOpenCompute for of LLVM-project. https://github.com/RadeonOpenCompute/llvm-project/tree/roc-4.3.x
15. SYCL. https://www.khronos.org/registry/SYCL
16. Thrust. https://thrust.github.io
17. Top500 entry: Fugaku, A64FX. https://www.top500.org/system/179807

18. Bussmann, M., et al.: Radiative signatures of the relativistic Kelvin-Helmholtz instability. In: Proceedings of the International Conference on High Performance Computing, Networking, Storage and Analysis, pp. 5:1–5:12. SC 2013, ACM, New York, NY, USA (2013). http://doi.acm.org/10.1145/2503210.2504564
19. Demidov, D., Ahnert, K., Rupp, K., Gottschling, P.: Programming CUDA and OpenCL: a case study using modern C++ libraries. SIAM J. Sci. Comput. **35**(5), 1–12 (2013). https://doi.org/10.1137/120903683. https://dblp.org/rec/journals/siamsc/DemidovARG13.bib
20. Dionne, L.: `std::tuple<>` should be trivially constructible, May 2019. https://cplusplus.github.io/LWG/issue3211
21. Edwards, H.C., Trott, C.R., Sunderland, D.: Kokkos: enabling manycore performance portability through polymorphic memory access patterns. J. Parallel Distrib. Comput. **74**(12), 3202–3216 (2014). https://doi.org/10.1016/j.jpdc.2014.07.003,http://www.sciencedirect.com/science/article/pii/S0743731514001257. (domain-Specific Languages and High-Level Frameworks for High-Performance Computing)
22. Juckeland, G., et al.: From describing to prescribing parallelism: translating the SPEC ACCEL OpenACC Suite to OpenMP target directives. In: Taufer, M., Mohr, B., Kunkel, J.M. (eds.) ISC High Performance 2016. LNCS, vol. 9945, pp. 470–488. Springer, Cham (2016). https://doi.org/10.1007/978-3-319-46079-6_33
23. Matthes, A., Widera, R., Zenker, E., Worpitz, B., Huebl, A., Bussmann, M.: Tuning and optimization for a variety of many-core architectures without changing a single line of implementation code using the Alpaka library. In: Kunkel, J.M., Yokota, R., Taufer, M., Shalf, J. (eds.) ISC High Performance 2017. LNCS, vol. 10524, pp. 496–514. Springer, Cham (2017). https://doi.org/10.1007/978-3-319-67630-2_36
24. Ozen, G., Lopez, G.: Accelerating Fortran DO CONCURRENT with GPUs and the NVIDIA HPC SDK. https://developer.nvidia.com/blog/accelerating-fortran-do-concurrent-with-gpus-and-the-nvidia-hpc-sdk/
25. Zenker, E., et al.: Alpaka - an abstraction library for parallel kernel acceleration. IEEE Computer Society, May 2016. http://arxiv.org/abs/1602.08477

Accelerating Quantum Many-Body Configuration Interaction with Directives

Brandon Cook[1](✉), Patrick J. Fasano[2]●, Pieter Maris[3], Chao Yang[4], and Dossay Oryspayev[5]

[1] National Energy Research Scientific Computing Center, Lawrence Berkeley National Laboratory, Berkeley, CA, USA
bgcook@lbl.gov
[2] Department of Physics, University of Notre Dame, Notre Dame, IN, USA
pfasano@nd.edu
[3] Department of Physics and Astronomy, Iowa State University, Ames, IA, USA
pmaris@iastate.edu
[4] Computational Research Division, Lawrence Berkeley National Laboratory, Berkeley, CA, USA
cyang@lbl.gov
[5] Computational Science Initiative, Brookhaven National Laboratory, Upton, NY, USA
doryspaye@bnl.gov

Abstract. Many-Fermion Dynamics—nuclear, or MFDn, is a configuration interaction (CI) code for nuclear structure calculations. It is a platform-independent Fortran 90 code using a hybrid MPI+X programming model. For CPU platforms the application has a robust and optimized OpenMP implementation for shared memory parallelism. As part of the NESAP application readiness program for NERSC's latest Perlmutter system, MFDn has been updated to take advantage of accelerators. The current mainline GPU port is based on OpenACC. In this work we describe some of the key challenges of creating an efficient GPU implementation. Additionally, we compare the support of OpenMP and OpenACC on AMD and NVIDIA GPUs.

Keywords: Fortran · GPUs · OpenACC · OpenMP · Accelerators · Nuclear Configuration Interaction

1 Introduction

Many-Fermion Dynamics—nuclear, or MFDn, is a configuration interaction (CI) code for *ab initio* nuclear physics calculations. It calculates the approximate many-body wave function of self-bound atomic nuclei, starting from two- and three-nucleon interactions. In these calculations, the nuclear many-body Hamiltonian is represented as a large sparse symmetric matrix in configuration space. The lowest eigenvalues of this matrix correspond to the energy levels of the low-lying spectrum, and the eigenvectors represent the corresponding many-body wave function.

© P. Maris, P.J. Fasano, Brookhaven Science Associates, LLC, and The Regents of the University of California, manager and operator of Lawrence Berkley National Laboratory, under exclusive license to Springer Nature Switzerland AG, part of Springer Nature 2022
S. Bhalachandra et al. (Eds.): WACCPD 2021, LNCS 13194, pp. 112–132, 2022.
https://doi.org/10.1007/978-3-030-97759-7_6

Table 1. Test platforms

	Cori GPU	Cori DGX	Spock
GPU	NVIDIA V100	NVIDIA A100	AMD MI100
CPU	Intel Skylake	AMD Rome	AMD Rome
GPUs per node	8	8	4
CPUs per node	2	2	1
Bus	PCIe 3.0	PCIe 4.0	PCIe 4.0
per GPU Memory	16 GB	40 GB	32 GB

Table 2. Compilers. Cray Fortran compiler version 12.0.1 claims full OpenACC 2.0 and partial OpenACC 2.6 support for Fortran.

Vendor	Version	_OPENACC	_OPENMP	V100	A100	MI100
NVIDIA	21.7	201711 (2.6)	202011 (5.1)	✓	✓	
HPE/Cray	12.0.1	201306 (2.0)	201511 (4.5)	✓		✓

MFDn is a platform-independent Fortran 90 code using a hybrid MPI+X programming model. Over the past decade, it has been successfully deployed on multi-core supercomputers such as Jaguar at the Oak Ridge Leadership Class Facility (OLCF), Mira at the Argonne Leadership Class Facility (ALCF), and Edison at the National Energy Research Scientific Computing Center (NERSC) using MPI + OpenMP [2,10,11,13]. Currently it is in production on many-core systems [4,5,7] such as Cori at NERSC and Theta at ALCF, as well as other supercomputers worldwide.

As part of the NESAP application readiness program for NERSC's latest Perlmutter system, MFDn is being updated to take advantage of accelerators. The current mainline GPU port uses OpenACC. In this work we consider several kernels that are representative for some of the most time-consuming parts of MFDn [5,12,16]. We describe some of the challenges and limitations of running them efficiently on GPUs with OpenMP and/or OpenACC directives, using both the NVIDIA and Cray Fortran compilers. We test their performance on NVIDIA V100 "Volta", NVIDIA A100 "Ampere", and AMD MI100 GPUs, as well as on Intel multi-core CPUs; see Table 1 for more details of the test systems.

We performed tests on Cori GPU (NVIDIA V100 GPUs) and Cori DGX (NVIDIA A100) with the NVIDIA compiler only, whereas our tests on Spock (AMD MI100) are performed with the Cray compiler only (see Table 2). The Cray compiler version 12.0 was not available for the Cori GPU system at the time of writing and it does not support NVIDIA A100 GPUs. All tests were done on exclusively-allocated nodes. In order to minimize any NUMA effects, tests on GPUs used a single GPU, while tests on CPUs used a single socket.

In our implementations we have primarily explored three models: OpenACC with `parallel` and `loop` directives, i. e., no `kernels` directives; OpenMP target offload with prescriptive style directives (`teams distribute parallel do`); and OpenMP target with the new `loop` construct introduced in OpenMP 5.0.

In all cases maintaining performance on CPUs and code maintainability was also a priority. The NVIDIA compiler claims support for OpenACC 2.6 with "many features" from 2.7 and for a subset of OpenMP 5.1, while the Cray Fortran compiler claims support for OpenACC 2.0 with "partial support" for 2.6 and full support OpenMP 4.5 with partial support for 5.0. We highlight where we encountered missing features or shortcomings throughout and in particular in architectural specialization in Sect. 2.3 and reductions on arrays in Sect. 2.4.

2 Computational Motifs in Configuration Interaction Code MFDn

The key computational challenges for MFDn are (1) efficient localization of the nonzero Hamiltonian matrix elements and evaluation of the corresponding matrix elements, and (2) efficient sparse matrix–vector and matrix–matrix products used in the solution of the eigenvalue problem, both while effectively using the available aggregate memory [5,12,16]. Figure 1 shows the overall structure of MFDn. The GPU port of the LOBPCG eigensolver [15] using OpenACC is described in [14]. In this work we concentrate on the matrix construction phase and the evaluation of observables, which each take up about one-quarter to one-third of the total runtime, while iterative eigensolving takes about one-third to one-half of the total runtime. In CI calculations, the many-body wave functions are approximated by an expansion in *many-body basis states*; in MFDn we use antisymmetrized products of single-particle states with quantum numbers (n, ℓ, j, m) (see, e.g., Ref. [17] for the meaning of these quantum numbers). The many-body basis states can then be characterized by the set of single-particle quantum numbers for each nucleon. It is convenient to group together many-body states with the same sets of values for the quantum numbers (n, ℓ, j), but different sets of values for the magnetic projection quantum numbers m. This grouping leads to a natural hierarchy in the sparsity structure of the Hamiltonian matrix, which in turn allows for efficient localization and evaluation of nonzero matrix elements. In addition, this grouping also facilitates an efficient block-diagonal preconditioner for the LOBPCG algorithm [15]. We refer to these groups of many-body states as *many-body basis orbitals*. To describe the sparsity structure, we furthermore define tiles as pairs of row and column many-body basis orbitals.

In order to efficiently locate the nonzero matrix elements we exploit this hierarchical structure, by first determining which tiles can contain nonzero matrix elements (lines 2 through 5 of Fig. 1) and next counting how many nonzero matrix elements there are (lines 6 through 8) in each tile. The actual construction of the sparse matrix starts in line 11, with the nonzero matrix elements and their location evaluated and stored in line 14 of Fig. 1. Note that the structure of the double loops starting in lines 2 and in line 7 is essentially the same; the corresponding motif is discussed in Sect. 2.1 below. Also the double loops starting in line 12 have a similar structure, except that in this case, the obtained results in the innermost loop are stored in an array; this motif is discussed in Sect. 2.3 below. (Note that this motif is also used implicitly in line 5 of Fig. 1).

1. Enumerate and distribute many-body basis orbitals (Ψ_j)
2. Loop over column orbitals (Ψ_m)
    Loop over row orbitals (Ψ_l)
3.   Compare the single-particle orbitals of Ψ_l and Ψ_m
         increment *tile_cnt* if up to $2d$ differences
    End Loop
    End Loop
4. Allocate arrays of length *tile_cnt* to store nonzero tiles (T_k)
5. Repeat 2 and store nonzero tiles ($T_k = (\Psi_l, \Psi_m)$):
    pairs of orbitals with up to $2d$ differences
6. Loop over tiles (($\Psi_l, \Psi_m) = T_k$)
7.   Loop over column states ($\Phi_j \in \Psi_m$)
      Loop over row states ($\Phi_i \in \Psi_l$)
8.   Compare the single-particle states of Φ_i and Φ_j
           increment cnt_k if up to $2d$ differences
        End Loop
      End Loop
    End Loop
9. Convert cnt_k's to $offset_k$'s
10. Allocate arrays of length $\sum cnt_k$ to store H_{ij}
11. Loop over tiles (($\Psi_l, \Psi_m) = T_k$)
12.   Loop over column states ($\Phi_j \in \Psi_m$)
       Loop over row states ($\Phi_i \in \Psi_l$)
13.   Compare the single-particle states of Φ_i and Φ_j
            cycle if more than $2d$ differences
14.   Compute the nonzero matrix entry H_{ij} and store
        End Loop
      End Loop
    End Loop
15. Obtain lowest n eigenvalues E and eigenvectors c of H_{ij}
    using distributed LOBPCG or Lanczos algorithm
16. Loop over tiles (($\Psi_l, \Psi_m) = T_k$)
17.   Loop over column states ($\Phi_j \in \Psi_m$)
       Loop over row states ($\Phi_i \in \Psi_l$)
18.   Compare the single-particle states of Φ_i and Φ_j
            cycle if more than $2d$ differences
19.   Compute m nonzero matrix elements $O_{ij}(1:m)$
20.   Update $a(1:n*m) = a(1:n*m) + c_i(1:n)*O_{ij}(1:m)*c_j(1:n)$
        End Loop
      End Loop
    End Loop

Fig. 1. Schematic outline of the structure of MFDn during the matrix construction phase (lines 2 through 14) and evaluation of physical observables (lines 16 through 20), for a d-body Hamiltonian and d-body operators for observables.

Once the nonzero matrix elements are evaluated and stored, we can obtain the lowest n eigenvalues and eigenvectors c using an iterative eigensolver. In MFDn we use either LOBPCG or a Lanczos algorithm with reorthogonalization, as indicated in line 15 of Fig. 1. Details of the GPU port of our LOBPCG eigensolver using OpenACC are described in Ref. [14].

Finally, in lines 16 through 20 of Fig. 1 we calculate m different physical observables using the coefficients c_i of the lowest n eigenvectors and m two-body operators. Typically, we use 8 or 16 eigenvectors, and up to $m \sim 16$ different operators corresponding to different observables. Note that lines 16 to 18 have the same structure as lines 11 to 13, but instead of storing the nonzero matrix elements of the operators, we contract them with the n eigenvectors. The corresponding motif for these loops is discussed in Sect. 2.4 below.

2.1   Matrix Sparsity Determination

A typical loop structure in the matrix construction phase, as well as in the evaluation of observables, is shown in Fig. 2. The (i, j)th entry of the many-body Hamiltonian with a d-body interaction, $H_{ij} = \langle \Phi_i | H | \Phi_j \rangle$, can only be nonzero if the many-body states Φ_i and Φ_j differ by at most $2d$ single-particle states. Thus, the first step in the matrix construction (and in the evaluation of observables given by the expectation value of a d-body operator) is to determine which matrix elements can be nonzero. This is done in line 3 of the loop; subsequently, lines 4 and 5 indicate the actual evaluation of the nonzero matrix entry, which can be stored in memory (see line 14 of Fig. 1), or directly used in a matrix–vector multiply or vector–matrix–vector contraction for the calculation of expectation values (see line 20 of Fig. 1). These are more complicated operations which are accomplished by separate (sequential) subroutine calls, the details of which are beyond the scope of this work.

---

1. Loop over column states (Φ_j)
2.   Loop over row states (Φ_i)
3.   Compare the single-particle states of Φ_i and Φ_j
           cycle if more than $2d$ differences
4.   (optional) Compute the nonzero matrix entry H_{ij} and store
5.   (optional) FMA of H_{ij} with ith row (and jth column) vector element
6.   End Loop
7. End Loop

Fig. 2. A typical loop structure in the matrix construction phase and during the evaluation of physical observables.

The localization of nonzero matrix elements involves determining which many-body basis states may be connected by the given particle rank (e. g., two-body) Hamiltonian. Given a single-particle basis with $n_{\text{s.p.}}$ single-particle states, a many-body basis state Φ_i for fermionic systems can be represented by a binary string of length $n_{\text{s.p.}}$, denoted by $\text{BIN}(\Phi_i)$, where each binary bit of $\text{BIN}(\Phi_i)$ indicates whether the corresponding single-particle state is occupied. The total number of particles in the many-body state Φ_i is the number of 1's in $\text{BIN}(\Phi_i)$, i.e., the population count $\text{popcount}(\text{BIN}(\Phi_i))$. Information regarding all differently-occupied single-particle states between two bit-representations $\text{BIN}(\Phi_i)$ and $\text{BIN}(\Phi_j)$ is encoded by $\text{BIN}(\Phi_i) \oplus \text{BIN}(\Phi_j)$, where $\oplus$ denotes the bit-wise exclusive-or operation. The number of differently-occupied single-particle states is then $\text{popcount}(\text{BIN}(\Phi_i) \oplus \text{BIN}(\Phi_j))$. If both bit-representations describe states with the same number of particles, then the number of differently-occupied single-particle states is always even; with a two-body potential, only many-body matrix elements with 0, 2, or 4 differently-occupied single-particle states can be nonzero. If there are more than four differently-occupied single-particle states the matrix element must be zero.

The storage requirements of such a bit representation is proportional to the number of single-particle states, but independent of the number of particles in the system. Alternatively, one can represent an N-body basis state Φ_i by an array or tuple of N short integers $\text{MBS}(a_1{:}a_N)$ with $a_1 < a_2 < \cdots < a_N$, where each element a_i indicates which single-particle state is occupied. The storage requirement of this method is proportional to N, the number of particles, but independent of the number of single-particle states $n_{\text{s.p.}}$. For a relatively small number of particles ($N \sim 10 - 20$ in MFDn), but a large ($n_{\text{s.p.}} \gtrsim 1{,}000$) number of single-particle states, the MBS representation is more advantageous in terms of memory than storing the states as a bit representation. However, determining the differently-occupied single-particle states is significantly more complex when Φ_i and Φ_j are in the MBS representation (see Listing 1). Note the factor of two to ensure consistent counts with the population count on the bit representation.

In MFDn the low-lying single-particle states are most likely to be occupied. For this reason we use a bit representation for the 64 lowest single-particle states, in combination with an array of N 16-bit integers $\text{MBS}(a_1{:}a_N)$ to store the full many-body state. This allows for efficient filtering of pairs of states with bit arithmetic on the most likely to be occupied states while incurring minimal additional storage overhead. Our OpenACC implementation of the algorithm used to count the number of different single-particle states by first performing a population count on the 64 lowest single-particle states, followed by a detailed comparison of the MBS representation if the population count is at most $2d$, is given in code Listings 1 and 2.

OpenMP prescriptive, OpenMP loop and OpenMP loop with bind hints directives for the first and second level of parallelism in Listing 2 are shown in Listings 3 and 4 respectively. The first level is typically mapped to cores on CPUs, thread blocks on NVIDIA GPUs and workgroups on AMD GPUs while the second level is typically mapped to SIMD lane(s) on CPUs, threads on NVIDIA GPUs and work items on AMD GPUs. Note that the comparison of the two complete many-body states is performed in a function (see Listing 1), which needs a `!$acc routine seq` directive so that the OpenACC loops in Listing 2 do indeed get parallelized; with

```
1   integer function count_difference(s1, n1, s2, n2)
2     integer, intent(in) :: n1, n2, s1(n1), s2(n2)
3     integer :: i1, i2, d, diffs1, diffs2
4     !$acc routine seq
5     i1 = 1
6     i2 = 1
7     diffs1 = 0
8     diffs2 = 0
9     do
10      if ( (i1 > n1) .or. (i2 > n2) ) exit
11      d = s1(i1) - s2(i2)
12      if (d < 0) then
13        diffs1 = diffs1 + 1
14        i1 = i1 + 1
15      else if (d > 0) then
16        diffs2 = diffs2 + 1
17        i2 = i2 + 1
18      else
19        i1 = i1 + 1
20        i2 = i2 + 1
21      end if
22    end do
23    count_difference = 2*max(diffs1, diffs2)
24  end function count_difference
```

Listing 1: Sequential function for detailed comparison of two many-body states.

```
1   !$acc parallel loop
2   do i = 1, n
3     c = 0
4     !$acc loop reduction(+:c)
5     do j = 1, n
6       d = popcnt(ieor(bitrep1(i), bitrep2(j)))
7       if (d > 4) cycle
8       d = count_difference(mbstate1(:,i), np, mbstate2(:,j), np)
9       if (d <= 4) c = c + 1
10    end do
11    !$acc end loop
12    counts(i) = c
13  end do
14  !$acc end parallel loop
15  numnnz = sum(counts)
```

Listing 2: Counting nonzero matrix elements with OpenACC, using both a bit representation for the first 64 single-particle states of Φ_i and Φ_j and a detailed comparison for the MBS representation if needed. The highlighted lines show the directives used for the two levels of parallelism.

```
1    !$acc parallel loop
2    !$omp target teams distribute private(d)
3    !$omp target teams loop private(d)
4    !$omp target teams loop bind(teams) private(d)
```

Listing 3: OpenACC, OpenMP prescriptive, OpenMP loop and OpenMP loop with hints directives to express the first level of parallelism highlighted in line 1 of Listing 2.

```
1    !$acc loop reduction(+:c)
2    !$omp parallel do reduction(+:c) private(d)
3    !$omp loop reduction(+:c) private(d)
4    !$omp loop bind(parallel) reduction(+:c) private(d)
```

Listing 4: OpenACC, OpenMP prescriptive, OpenMP loop and OpenMP loop with hints directives to express the second level of parallelism highlighted in line 4 of Listing 2.

OpenMP there is no need for a similar directive when the routine is defined in the same compilation unit, though !$omp declare target may be used when this is not the case.

For our performance tests we used many-body states with 4, 8, 12, 16 and 20 particles, 128 single-particle states, and a bit representation based on only the lowest 64 single-particle states. We randomly generated many-body states biased towards the lowest states, and counted the number of nonzero matrix elements for a two-body interaction. We present in Figs. 3 and 4 results with 8 particles as the density of nonzeros (median density was 6×10^{-6}) most closely represents the regime of interest for MFDn. Note that fewer particles with the state generation scheme correspond to more nonzero elements and more particles result in fewer nonzero elements. For comparison and correctness, we also ran two additional versions: a version without the popcount on the bit representation, as well as a version with a complete bit representation of all 128 single-particle states and using exclusively the popcount on this extended bit representation.

Figure 4 shows the performance of the bit representation and combined versions of the counting routines on MI100 and A100 GPUs implemented with OpenACC and OpenMP. On NVIDIA and AMD GPUs the OpenACC directives provide the best performance in most cases. In several instances there were performance issues when a function or subroutine call was introduced: particularly with OpenMP, usually manifest as a failure to generate parallel code for the second level of parallelism. In the case of !$omp loop directives we found that it was necessary to include bind annotations to recover the performance obtained by the OpenACC implementations on NVIDIA GPUs. The performance difference between all versions and implementations is shown in Fig. 3. On NVIDIA platforms we found there is overhead associated with OpenMP with prescriptive !$omp target teams

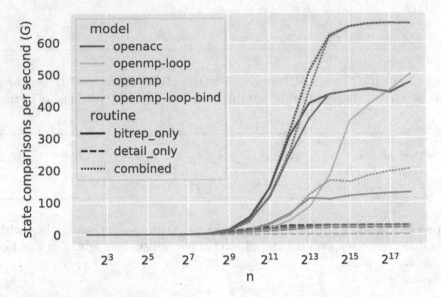

Fig. 3. Performance of interacting state counting routines on A100 with 8 particles (median density of nonzero elements is $\sim 6 \times 10^{-6}$). The vertical axis shows the number of state comparisons made per second, rate $= n^2/\text{time}$ (higher is better).

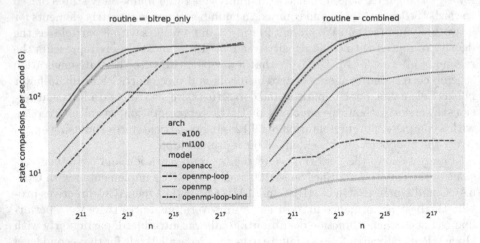

Fig. 4. Performance of bit representation only and combined interacting state counting routines on A100 and MI100 with 8 particles (median density of nonzero elements is 0.000006). The vertical axis shows the number of state comparisons made per second, rate $= n^2/\text{time}$ (higher is better).

distribute and !$omp parallel do directives compared to the !$omp loop directives. The compiler parallelizes on both teams and threads, but shows reduced performance. This is likely due to the additional semantic constraints for the !$omp parallel directive introducing some overhead in code generated by the compiler.

2.2   Parallel Prefix Sum

On multi-core CPUs, it is often convenient to use private arrays – and as long as there is sufficient memory, there is no intrinsic limitation on the private array size. In practice, it is limited by the OMP_STACKSIZE which the user can increase from its default value if necessary. Further, the use of thread-private arrays can often result in good performance as it helps ensure cache locality on CPUs. However, the situation on GPUs is different. Although private arrays can be used in both OpenACC and with OpenMP offload, there are more limitations on the size of such private arrays and/or on the number of gangs/teams or vector length one can use, due to the order of magnitude more parallelism available in GPUs. In particular in inner loops, private arrays should be avoided or limited to small arrays with only a handful of array elements; and even at the gang/team level, large arrays with (tens of) thousands of array elements severely limits the number of gangs/teams one can use.

In order to reduce (or better, completely avoid) the need for private arrays, it can be useful to convert counts, such as the counts of nonzero matrix elements discussed in Sect. 2.1, into offsets, so that one can use a single large shared array with appropriate offsets, instead of many allocatable private arrays. Specifically, converting counts x_i into offsets y_i can be implemented as

$$y_{i+1} = \sum_{j=0}^{i} x_j = y_i + x_i \tag{1}$$

with $y_1 = 0$, and is often referred to as a prefix sum or cumulative sum or scan. Here we focus on addition of integers, but in general only a binary associative operator is required.

On CPUs this operation is fast, and furthermore OpenMP 5.0 introduced a scan directive that extends reductions. However, this feature is not currently supported for GPUs by the compilers tested in this work. OpenACC provides no equivalent directive. We note that production quality implementations of this operation

```
1  !$acc serial present (x,y)
2   y(1) = 0
3   do i = 1, n-1
4     y(i+1) = y(i) + x(i)
5   end do
6  !$acc end serial
```

Listing 5: Serial prefix sum with OpenACC.

Algorithm 1. Work-efficient parallel prefix sum (Algos. 3 and 4 of Ref. [8])

1: **for** $p \leftarrow 0, \log_2 n - 1$ **do**   ▷ sweep up (or reduce)
2:     **for** $j \leftarrow 0, n - 1$ by 2^{p+1} **do**   ▷ parallel
3:         $y\left(j + 2^{p+1}\right) \leftarrow y\left(j + 2^p\right) + y\left(j + 2^{p+1}\right)$
4:     **end for**
5: **end for**
6: $x(n) \leftarrow 0$
7: **for** $p \leftarrow \log_2 n, 0$ **do**   ▷ sweep down
8:     **for** $j \leftarrow 0, n - 1$ by 2^{p+1} **do**   ▷ parallel
9:         $tmp \leftarrow y\left(j + 2^p\right)$
10:         $y\left(j + 2^p\right) \leftarrow y\left(j + 2^{p+1}\right)$
11:         $y\left(j + 2^{p+1}\right) \leftarrow tmp + y\left(j + 2^{p+1}\right)$
12:     **end for**
13: **end for**

---

may be available in C++ libraries such as Thrust [6] or Kokkos [1], but that including C++ or vendor specific frameworks in a Fortran code with a goal of portability introduces significant maintenance costs. In many cases it is preferable to avoid data transfers between the host and accelerator, even at the cost of inefficient use of the device. With OpenACC's `!$acc serial` directive a potentially expensive data transfer can be avoided as shown in Listing 5. Generally one should consider a performance model that includes bandwidth between host and device, performance on either host and device and the potential for any latency/blocking effects introduced by the data motion when considering an implementation.

For prefix sums over large sequences, a parallel implementation can realize significant speedups. We note that in MFDn the offsets can be reused many times so that the overall impact for the application run time is small, but this common primitive can be found in many applications [3]. A work-efficient algorithm for a parallel scan is shown in Algorithm 1 - the work-efficient algorithm consists of an up and down sweep [3,8]. The main idea is to sweep up and down a binary tree of the input data. The "up" or "reduce" sweep proceeds from the leaves to the root, computing partial sums in place. In the "down" sweep phase the binary tree is traversed from the last element down (root) to the leaves.

An implementation of Algorithm 1 in OpenACC is shown in Listing 6. As written it assumes power of two arrays; non-power of two arrays can be padded with zeros. We note that there are many possible further optimizations and refer interested readers to Refs. [3,8]. In OpenACC, each `parallel` region will result in a new kernel launch, but with the `async` clause we can queue them all in non-blocking manner and rely that they will be executed in order. A similar approach can be implemented in OpenMP with `nowait` and `depend` clauses. Figure 5 shows the performance of serial and parallel prefix sum with OpenACC on A100, V100, and Skylake. Unfortunately the Cray compiler's partial support for OpenACC 2.6 does not include the `serial` directive so we do not include MI100 results for these implementations. For large arrays on A100 GPUs the parallel implementation can be over 500× faster than a serial implementation. This demonstrates the importance

```
1    !$acc data present (x,y)
2    !$acc parallel loop async
3    do j = 1, n
4      y(j) = x(j)
5    end do
6    !$acc end parallel
7    offset = 1
8    ! sweep up, reduction in place
9    do while (offset < n)
10     !$acc parallel loop firstprivate(offset) present(y) async
11     do concurrent (j=0:n-1:2*offset)
12       y(j + 2*offset) = y(j + offset) + y(j + 2*offset)
13     end do
14     !$acc end parallel
15     offset = 2*offset
16   end do
17   ! sweep down, complete the scan
18   !$acc serial async
19   y(n) = 0
20   !$acc end serial
21   offset = rshift(offset, 1)
22   do while(offset > 0)
23     !$acc parallel loop firstprivate(offset, tmp) present(y) async
24     do concurrent(j=0:n-1:2*offset) local(tmp)
25       tmp = y(j + offset)
26       y(j + offset) = y(j + 2*offset)
27       y(j + 2*offset) = tmp + y(j + 2*offset)
28     end do
29     !$acc end parallel
30     offset = rshift(offset, 1)
31   end do
32   !$acc wait
33   !$acc end data
```

Listing 6: Parallel scan with OpenACC corresponding to Algorithm 1

of support for serial work on accelerators (and corresponding constructs) for productivity, support for asynchronous work for performance and the desirability of a good language/library support for parallel primitives such as prefix sums.

2.3   Filling Shared Arrays

After an initial pass to obtain the nonzero counts and offsets as described in Sects. 2.1 and 2.2 a second pass is often performed to store relevant information such as a row or column index, or the nonzero value, into a global (shared) array, see e.g. line 14 of Fig. 1. Since we are using a multilevel hierarchical structure for the sparse matrix, this motif appears in several situations, not only for the matrix

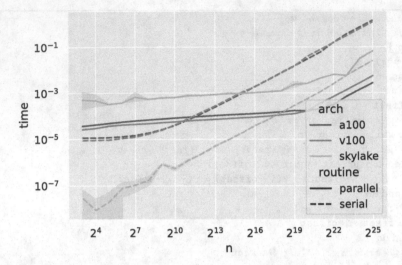

Fig. 5. Performance of prefix sum implemented with OpenACC on different architectures in parallel and serial (lower is better).

elements themselves. Generally there are two levels of parallelism: an outer loop, with no data dependencies, and an inner loop, where order does not matter but there is a dependency. The outer loop alone typically has enough parallelism to saturate a CPU but not a GPU.

On GPUs, OpenACC directives can be used to efficiently implement such a motif as shown in Listing 7. Equivalent directives are available in OpenMP. The `!$acc atomic capture` directive ensures that the value of the shared array element `indx(i)` gets incremented by one and assigned to the local (private) variable `k`, which can then be used as an index for filling the desired array with the appropriate value. On GPUs the performance penalty attributed to atomic operation in the inner loop is rather modest, and the exposed parallelism of the inner loop overwhelms this penalty, resulting in significant speedup over CPUs as shown in Fig. 6.

The same source code can also be compiled for and run on CPUs. On CPUs, when the parallelism available in the outermost level is sufficient, we can indicate that the inner loop should be sequential with the addition of the `!$acc device_type(host) seq` clauses. Unfortunately, the OpenACC specification does not support the `!$acc device_type` clause on `!$acc atomic` constructs. The performance of Listing 7 on multiple architectures is shown in Fig. 6. With the atomic operation explicitly in the inner loop, this implementation performs worse on CPUs than necessary despite there being no contention between threads on the atomic operations due to the overhead of atomic semantics. In OpenMP 5.0 `metadirective` was introduced to support this use case, but compiler support is not available at the time of writing. In principle, `declare variant` in OpenMP or runtime calls in OpenACC to selectively choose between multiple subroutine

```
1    !$acc parallel loop
2    do i = 1, n
3      indx(i) = offset(i)
4      !$acc loop device_type(host) seq
5      do j = 1, m
6        if (mod(j,p) == 0) then
7          !$acc atomic capture
8          indx(i) = indx(i) + 1
9          k = indx(i)
10         !$acc end atomic
11         arr(k) = j
12       end if
13     end do
14   end do
15   !$acc end parallel
```

Listing 7: Filling shared arrays on GPUs using OpenACC.

versions could be used to enable performance on CPUs and GPUs with a single source at the expense of code duplication. Otherwise use of the preprocessor would be required.

2.4 Array Reductions

Finally, to compute physical observables one needs to calculate the expectation values of the corresponding operators O_k (see line 20 of Fig. 1):

$$a_k = \sum_{ij} x_i \, (O_k)_{ij} \, y_j \,. \tag{2}$$

In practice this requires a reduction of an array with a small number of elements. In the context of the MFDn application the array is typically of dimension $m \in [8, 256]$. Here we consider a simplified version of the motif (shown in Listing 8) that omits the check if two many-body states interact and any computation of additional physical matrix elements in order to explore programming model support

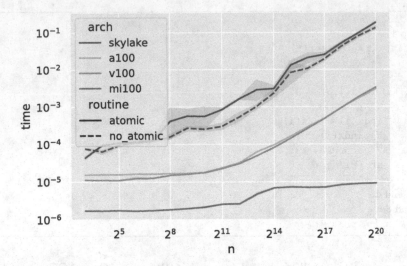

Fig. 6. Performance of filling a shared array with OpenACC (Listing 7) with $m = 512$ and $p = 1$ on MI100, A100, V100 and Skylake (lower is better).

for the motif. In this application trading memory for performance as in [9] is undesirable since it will limit scaling to large problems on full systems. We consider 3 implementations for "small" array reductions:

- reduction clauses with array arguments;
- atomic updates to individual array elements;
- generating a scalar reduction for each element of the array with fypp.

Direct Array Reduction Support. Both the OpenACC 2.7+ and OpenMP 4.5+ specifications support arrays as arguments to reduction clauses in directives. However, compiler support for these features varies. With OpenACC, the Cray compiler only provides partial OpenACC 2.6 support and array reductions were not introduced until 2.7. The NVIDIA compiler also does not support arrays in reduction clauses with OpenACC. With OpenMP both Cray and NVIDIA compilers support array reductions. However, this feature was only introduced in NVIDIA's 21.7 release. With Cray the compiler warns, "An OpenMP teams construct with an array reduction is limited to a single team." With OpenMP, the NVIDIA compiler encounters a run time error as the array size is increased, or fails to compile when managed memory is used. Figure 7 shows the performance of array reduction on A100, MI100 and Skylake CPUs respectively where supported. Performance of array reductions was only competitive with other solutions on Skylake.

```
1   !$acc parallel loop collapse(2) reduction(+:a)
2   do i = 1, n
3     do j = 1, n
4       do k = 1, m
5         a(k) = a(k) + x(k,i) * y(k,j)
6       end do
7     end do
8   end do
9   !$acc end parallel
```

Listing 8: Array reduction: array variable in a `reduction` clause.

```
1   !$acc parallel loop collapse(3)
2   do i = 1, n
3     do j = 1, n
4       do k = 1, m
5         !$acc atomic
6         a(k) = a(k) + x(k,i) * y(k,j)
7         !$acc end atomic
8       end do
9     end do
10  end do
11  !$acc end parallel
```

Listing 9: Array reduction: atomic updates

Array Reduction with Atomics. With atomic constructs we are able to compile a single version for all architectures. Compared to the case in Sect. 2.3 where there is no contention, when $n \gg m$, the contention is quite high which results in a significant performance penalty compared to an optimized reduction algorithm on the Skylake CPU as seen in the top panel of Fig. 7. Our results indicate that the implementation shown in Listing 9 can achieve reasonable performance on GPUs but not CPUs. We also note that there is an additional danger with the use of `collapse` with many loops, the combined iteration space may manifest a integer overflow for realistic array sizes if 32 bit integers are used as loop indices even though no individual loop overflows in a serial implementation.

Generated Scalar Reductions. In the case of small arrays another approach is to use a preprocessor that enables templating and metaprogramming such as `fypp` to generate routines that implement a scalar reduction for each element of the array as in Listings 10 and 11. As shown in Fig. 7 this approach achieves good performance on all architectures. However, this approach works for small arrays, but as array size is increased runs into several issues either with directive line length (NVIDIA) or compiler register allocation routines (HPE/Cray). Further it can result in significant undesirable cognitive and compilation time overhead. In sum-

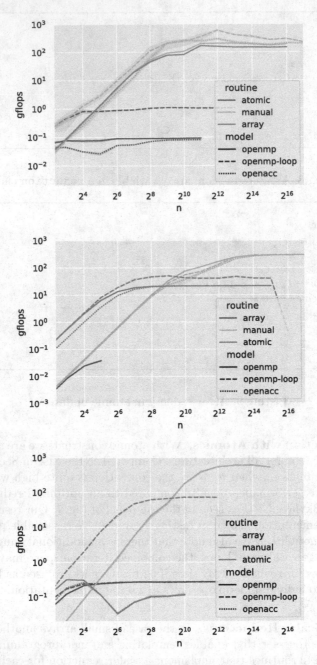

Fig. 7. Performance of array reduction with array size of 64 (higher is better). *Top:* On Skylake CPUs; *Middle:* On A100, where we encountered run time errors for $n > 2^5$ with OpenMP array reduction and a compile error with OpenMP with loops; *Bottom:* On MI100, where for $mn^2 \geq 2^{32}$ there appears to be a correctness error due to integer overflow on the collapsed loops with the Cray compiler.

```
1   #:def CSV(x,n)
2   ${",".join(f"{x}{i}" for i in range(1, n+1))}$
3   #:enddef CSV
4   #:for num_elements in range(2, max_elements+1)
5     subroutine reduction${num_elements}$(x, y, a, n, dt)
6       integer, parameter :: m = ${num_elements}$
7       integer, intent(in) :: n
8       real(sp), dimension(m, n), intent(in) :: x, y
9       real(sp), intent(out) :: a(m)
10      integer :: i,j
11      real(dp) :: t0
12      real(dp), intent(out) :: dt
13  #:for i in range(1, num_elements+1)
14      real(sp) :: a${i}$
15  #:endfor
16      !$acc data present(x,y)
17      t0 = wtime()
18  #:for i in range(1, num_elements+1)
19      a${i}$ = a(${i}$)
20  #:endfor
21      !$acc parallel loop collapse(2) &
22      !$acc reduction(+:${CSV("a",num_elements)}$)
23      do i = 1, n
24        do j = 1, n
25  #:for i in range(1, num_elements+1)
26          a${i}$ = a${i}$ + x(${i}$,i) * y(${i}$,j)
27  #:endfor
28        end do
29      end do
30      !$acc end parallel
31  #:for i in range(1, num_elements+1)
32      a(${i}$) = a${i}$
33  #:endfor
34      dt = wtime() - t0
35      !$acc end data
36    end subroutine reduction${num_elements}$
37
38  #:endfor
```

Listing 10: Template code for generating reductions with **fypp**. Listing 11 shows a routine generated for $m = 3$.

mary no one method for array reductions is best in all situations, but in this case the manually generated reductions on scalars with OpenACC give the best overall cross-platform performance.

```
1    subroutine reduction3(x, y, a, n, dt)
2      integer, parameter :: m = 3
3      integer, intent(in) :: n
4      real(sp), dimension(m, n), intent(in) :: x, y
5      real(sp), intent(out) :: a(m)
6      integer :: i,j
7      real(dp) :: t0
8      real(dp), intent(out) :: dt
9      real(sp) :: a1
10     real(sp) :: a2
11     real(sp) :: a3
12     !$acc data present(x,y)
13     t0 = wtime()
14     a1 = a(1)
15     a2 = a(2)
16     a3 = a(3)
17     !$acc parallel loop collapse(2) &
18     !$acc reduction(+:a1,a2,a3)
19     do i = 1, n
20       do j = 1, n
21         a1 = a1 + x(1,i) * y(1,j)
22         a2 = a2 + x(2,i) * y(2,j)
23         a3 = a3 + x(3,i) * y(3,j)
24       end do
25     end do
26     !$acc end parallel
27     a(1) = a1
28     a(2) = a2
29     a(3) = a3
30     dt = wtime() - t0
31     !$acc end data
32   end subroutine reduction3
```

Listing 11: Routine for $m = 3$ case generated by fypp code in Listing 10.

3   Conclusion and Outlook

We highlighted several important features of programming for accelerators with directives that were key for an efficient GPU accelerated port of MFDn. Further we explored the performance implications of these modifications with CPUs and with multiple GPU and compiler vendors.

Avoiding use of private arrays in a production application that has undergone several years of optimization for multicore CPU platforms was a key challenge. The conversion of counts to offsets followed by indexing of shared array in a way that preserves CPU performance while enabling GPU offload was a key pattern that involved restructuring of many key data structures and routines in the application.

Our key points for application developers can be summarized as: avoid private arrays; check compiler diagnostic output to ensure parallel code is in fact generated; carefully check correctness along with performance; and be mindful of atomic operations when developing single source code for CPU and GPU architectures.

Our findings have shown several shortcomings of both the OpenACC and OpenMP specification/implementation with respect to specialization of code for different architectures that can hopefully be addressed in future editions of those specifications and compilers. Finally, we have identified several areas and motifs that compiler vendors may use to improve their products.

Acknowledgements. This work is supported by the U.S. Department of Energy (DOE) under Award Nos. DE-FG02-95ER40934 and DE-SC0018223 (SciDAC/NUCLEI), and by the DOE Office of Science, Office of Workforce Development for Teachers and Scientists, Office of Science Graduate Student Research (SCGSR) program (administered by the Oak Ridge Institute for Science and Education (ORISE), managed by ORAU under contract number DE-SC0014664).

This research used resources of the National Energy Research Scientific Computing Center (NERSC), a DOE Office of Science User Facility located at Lawrence Berkeley National Laboratory, operated under Contract No. DE-AC02-05CH11231, as well as resources of the Oak Ridge Leadership Computing Facility at the Oak Ridge National Laboratory, which is supported by the DOE Office of Science under Contract No. DE-AC05-00OR22725.

References

1. Bell, N., Hoberock, J.: Thrust: a productivity-oriented library for CUDA. In: Hwu, W.M.W. (ed.) GPU Computing Gems Jade Edition. Applications of GPU Computing Series, pp. 359–371. Morgan Kaufmann, Boston (2012). https://doi.org/10.1016/B978-0-12-385963-1.00026-5
2. Binder, S., Calci, A., Epelbaum, E., et al.: Few-nucleon systems with state-of-the-art chiral nucleon-nucleon forces. Phys. Rev. C **93**(4), 044002 (2016). https://doi.org/10.1103/PhysRevC.93.044002
3. Blelloch, G.E.: Prefix sums and their applications. Technical report CMU-CS-90-190, School of Computer Science, Carnegie Mellon University, November 1990. http://www.cs.cmu.edu/~scandal/papers/CMU-CS-90-190.html
4. Caprio, M.A., Fasano, P.J., Maris, P., McCoy, A.E.: Quadrupole moments and proton-neutron structure in p-shell mirror nuclei. Phys. Rev. C **104**(3), 034319034319 (2021). https://doi.org/10.1103/PhysRevC.104.034319
5. Cook, B., et al.: High performance optimizations for nuclear physics code MFDn on KNL. In: Taufer, M., Mohr, B., Kunkel, J.M. (eds.) ISC High Performance 2016. LNCS, vol. 9945, pp. 366–377. Springer, Cham (2016). https://doi.org/10.1007/978-3-319-46079-6_26
6. Edwards, H.C., Trott, C.R., Sunderland, D.: Kokkos: enabling manycore performance portability through polymorphic memory access patterns. J. Parallel Distrib. Comput. **74**(12), 3202–3216 (2014). https://doi.org/10.1016/j.jpdc.2014.07.003
7. Epelbaum, E., et al.: Few- and many-nucleon systems with semilocal coordinate-space regularized chiral two- and three-body forces. Phys. Rev. C **99**(2), 024313 (2019). https://doi.org/10.1103/PhysRevC.99.024313

8. Harris, M., Sengupta, S., Owens, J.D.: Parallel prefix sum (scan) with CUDA. In: GPU Gems, vol. 3, pp. 851–876. Addison-Wesley Professional (2007). Chap. 39

9. Kim, J.Y., Kang, J.S., Joh, M.: GPU acceleration of MPAS microphysics WSM6 using OpenACC directives: performance and verification. Comput. Geosci. **146**, 104627 (2021). https://doi.org/10.1016/j.cageo.2020.104627

10. Maris, P., Caprio, M.A., Vary, J.P.: Emergence of rotational bands in ab initio no-core configuration interaction calculations of the Be isotopes. Phys. Rev. C **91**(1), 014310 (2015). https://doi.org/10.1103/PhysRevC.91.014310

11. Maris, P., Vary, J.P., Navratil, P., et al.: Origin of the anomalous long lifetime of ^{14}C. Phys. Rev. Lett. **106**(20), 202502 (2011). https://doi.org/10.1103/PhysRevLett.106.202502

12. Maris, P., Aktulga, H.M., Binder, S., et al.: No core CI calculations for light nuclei with chiral 2- and 3-body forces. J. Phys: Conf. Ser. **454**, 012063 (2013). https://doi.org/10.1088/1742-6596/454/1/012063

13. Maris, P., Vary, J.P.: Ab initio nuclear structure calculations of p-shell nuclei with JISP16. Int. J. Mod. Phys. E **22**, 1330016 (2013). https://doi.org/10.1142/S0218301313300166

14. Maris, P., Yang, C., Oryspayev, D., Cook, B.: Accelerating an iterative eigensolver for nuclear structure configuration interaction calculations on GPUs using OpenACC (2021). http://arxiv.org/abs/2109.00485

15. Shao, M., Aktulga, H., Yang, C., et al.: Accelerating nuclear configuration interaction calculations through a preconditioned block iterative eigensolver. Comput. Phys. Commun. **222**, 1–13 (2018). https://doi.org/10.1016/j.cpc.2017.09.004

16. Sternberg, P., Ng, E.G., Yang, C., et al.: Accelerating configuration interaction calculations for nuclear structure. In: Proceedings of the 2008 ACM/IEEE Conference on Supercomputing. SC 2008. IEEE Press (2008). https://doi.org/10.5555/1413370.1413386

17. Suhonen, J.: From Nucleons to Nucleus: Concepts of Microscopic Nuclear Theory. Theoretical and Mathematical Physics, Springer, Berlin (2007). https://doi.org/10.1007/978-3-540-48861-3

GPU Offloading of a Large-Scale Gyrokinetic Particle-in-Cell Fortran Code on Summit: From OpenACC to OpenMP

Qiheng Cai[1]([✉]), Junyi Cheng[1], Yang Chen[1], Marcus Wagner[2], Christopher Daley[3], Dossay Oryspayev[4], Stefan Tirkas[1], Sophie Redd[1], and Scott Parker[1]

[1] University of Colorado at Boulder, Boulder, CO 80309, USA
qica3033@colorado.edu
[2] Hewlett Packard Enterprise, Houston, TX 77070, USA
[3] Lawrence Berkeley National Laboratory, Berkeley, CA 94720, USA
[4] Computational Science Initiative, Brookhaven National Laboratory, Upton, NY 11973, USA

Abstract. GPU offloading of a large-scale gyrokinetic particle-in-cell Fortran code is converted from using OpenACC to using OpenMP. Particle pushing and deposition are completely offloaded to GPU. Performance is compared between CPU and GPU, and between OpenACC and OpenMP. Good weak scaling (increasing particle number with fixed grid number) is obtained. Issues encountered when porting OpenMP GPU offloading are discussed.

Keywords: OpenMP GPU offloading · OpenACC GPU offloading · particle-in-cell

1 Introduction

We report the performance of a gyrokinetic Particle-in-Cell (PIC) code on GPUs using OpenMP offloading. PIC simulations are widely used to simulate plasma kinetic phenomena. In a PIC simulation, the trajectories of a large number of charged particles (ions and electrons) are followed numerically by integrating the equation of motion of charged particles in electromagnetic fields. The fields are determined by the plasma density and current via Maxwell's equations. Fields are usually represented on a set of spatial grids, and evaluated at the particle location via interpolation. A PIC simulation consists of three main components: the pushers, deposition and the field solvers. The pushers advance the particle phase-space coordinates in a time step. Deposition refers to the procedure by which the plasma density and current on the grids are obtained from the particles. The field solvers solve the Poisson equation and the Ampere equation to yield the electromagnetic fields. In a conventional PIC simulation the phase-space of particles is six-dimensional, three in space and three in velocity. In a strongly magnetized plasma such as that in a tokamak, charged particles gyrate

© Springer Nature Switzerland AG 2022
S. Bhalachandra et al. (Eds.): WACCPD 2021, LNCS 13194, pp. 133–148, 2022.
https://doi.org/10.1007/978-3-030-97759-7_7

around the magnetic field due to the Lorentz force. The Larmor radius of an ion is typically orders of magnitude smaller than the device size. This feature makes it possible to describe the plasma as consisting of gyro-rings, thereby reducing the dimensionality of the phase-space from six to five. Small scale turbulent fluctuations, on the ion Larmor radius scale, can be accounted for by gyro-averaging their effects on the gyro-ring. This leads to the gyrokinetic model of a plasma, and gyrokinetic simulation has become a widely used tool in magnetic confinement fusion research.

In a PIC simulation particles interact with each other mainly through the electromagnetic (EM) fields, and there is no explicit dependence among particles at the pusher step. This makes the pushers in a PIC simulation an ideal candidate for efficient parallelization and GPU offloading.

GEM is a gyrokinetic PIC code, written in FORTRAN, for tokamak plasma simulations. Multiple ion species (e.g. deuterium and tritium in a D-T reactor) and an electron species are followed in GEM. The electrons move along the field line much faster than the ions, which usually causes numerical difficulties in a PIC code. To overcome these difficulties a split-weight scheme [1,6] is used for the electrons. An additional field equation, which is the time derivative of the Poisson equation, is solved in the split-weight scheme. GEM uses the field-line-following coordinates [2] for both particle pushing and field solving. The primary domain decomposition is along the magnetic field line. The field equation is first Fourier transformed in the toroidal direction, then solved for each Fourier component. At present, the field equations for all the toroidal components are parallelized with OpenMP threading on CPU, and particles are also distributed among all the threads. In this work we report GPU offloading of the particle pushing and deposition. Offloading the field solvers to GPU is more challenging and will be undertaken in future.

Currently, the two most commonly used directive-based Application Programming Interfaces (APIs) are OpenACC and OpenMP. OpenACC provided many application developers a preview for directive-based programming for accelerators. This was followed by the development of the OpenMP specification Versions 4.0 and 4.5 in 2013 and 2015, respectively, which includes different types of parallelism such as SIMD, tasks, offloading, worksharing, etc. The difference between these two APIs are described in Larrea et al. [7]. Generally, OpenACC tends to be more descriptive, which means that compilers determine how a code for a particular target is parallelized. Alternatively, OpenMP 4.5 is developed as a prescriptive programming model and requires programmers to specifically determine the way to parallelize the code. Since performance-portability might be decreased by this prescriptive approach, OpenMP 5.0 introduced the loop directive to guarantee that concurrent execution of a loop is safe and to enable the compiler to apply more architecture-specific optimizations.

The Whole Device Model Application (WDMAPP) project launched by the Department of Energy's (DOE) Exascale Computing Program (ECP) aims to develop a first-principles-based computational tool for simulating both the core and the edge of a tokamak. Ku et al. [4,5] used OpenMP and OpenACC to develop the edge gyrokinetic code XGC. Recently, Cheng et al. [3] coupled the two PIC gyrokinetic codes GEM and XGC, GEM for the core region and XGC for the edge region. OpenACC is used for GPU-acceleration of GEM. It is desirable to assess performance gains from using GPUs and also to compare GEM GPU performance using OpenACC and OpenMP. This is the work undertaken in this paper.

This paper is organized as follows. The details of the experimental setup and conversion from OpenACC to OpenMP is presented in Sect. 2. The structure of the GEM code and related PIC procedures are presented in Sect. 3. In Sect. 4, the results comparing GPU vs CPU, OpenMP vs OpenACC for a single node, a multi-node scaling study, and sensitivity to CPU hardware threads are presented and analyzed. Discussion on remaining problems and possible solutions are provided in Sect. 5. Finally, a summary is given in Sect. 6.

2   Software and Experimental Setup

2.1   Experimental Setup

The performance of GEM is studied on Summit at OLCF. The hardware details of this supercomputer are illustrated in Table 1. As an IBM system available at OLCF, Summit contains 4608 compute nodes. Each node uses two IBM POWER9 CPUs with 22 cores running at 3.07 GHz and six NVIDIA Tesla V100 GPUs. Additionally, 512 GB of DDR4 memory are accessed by the POWER9 processors while 96 GB of High Bandwidth Memory (HBM2) are utilized by the V100 accelerators. The theoretical peak performance is 200,795 TFlop/s, and its Linpack performance is 148,600 TFlop/s. In addition, the NVIDIA compilers (e.g., NVFORTRAN, NVC++, and NVC) support not only directive-based programming of NVIDIA GPUs using OpenACC but also a subset of the OpenMP APIs for CPUs and GPUs. If an OpenMP application is properly structured for GPUs, which means that massive parallelism is exposed and no or little synchronization in segments of GPU-side code is implemented, the application should compile and execute with performance almost equivalent to that of OpenACC. Herein, on Summit, we use the latest version of the NVIDIA compilers, named NVIDIA HPC SDK 21.7, to compile OpenACC and OpenMP versions of the GEM code.

Table 1. Hardware details of a Summit's compute node.

	Summit
GPUs	6 × 16 GB NVIDIA Tesla V100
CPUs	2 × IBM POWER9 (AC922)
Cores	2 × 22 @ 3.07 GHz
CPU-GPU interconnect	NVlink 2.0

2.2   OpenMP GPU Offloading

Offloading code to accelerators is a significant capability introduced in OpenMP 4.0. Since then, heterogeneous computation has been under intensive development. As a directive-based programming model, OpenMP provides important `target` and `target teams` constructs to indicate the code regions to be offloaded to accelerator devices. Additionally, directives related to data allocation and deletion, data copy back and forth between CPU and GPU are provided by OpenMP. In this section, the details of the porting and optimization strategy and the baseline OpenMP GPU offloading implementation of GEM is described.

Porting and Optimization Strategy. GEM consists of four main parts: particle pushers, shift, deposition and field solvers. The primary domain decomposition is along the z-direction in the field-line-following coordinates. The z-direction is divided into equally spaced grids, and MPI tasks are assigned to each z-grid. An MPI process only holds those particles with a z-coordinate inside its z-grid. After particles are pushed, they are sorted into corresponding MPI processes (shifting). The pushers and the deposition subroutines mainly consist of loops over all the particles. The starting point for OpenMP offloading is the version of GPU offloading using OpenACC [3]. OpenMP GPU offloading is accomplished by converting the OpenACC directives to corresponding OpenMP directives with correct data movement. A general guideline for offloading a PIC code is to perform as much individual particle operation as possible on the GPU, such as pushing and deposition. For this purpose, all particle data and field data should be kept on GPU.

At present the MPI communication in the shifting step is performed on the CPU. This requires data movement between GPU and CPU. To reduce data movement, information of those particles that need to be moved across MPI processes is gathered on GPU, and only the data for these particles are updated between CPU and GPU [3]. Shifting consists of the initialization step and the actual data movement. The initialization step, which is called only once per shifting operation, constructs sorted pointers to particle holes and buffers for the sending and receiving processes. The actual data movement consists of nonblocking MPI communication, removal of holes, and reconstruction of particle arrays. This procedure is called for each particle array. In the shifting procedure, searching for nonhole indices from the end of the array in sequential order is more efficient than constructing the pointers to particle holes in a strictly increasing order. We have modified the initialization step to enable as many loops as possible to run on GPU.

Baseline OpenMP GPU Offloading Implementation in GEM. In order to execute a combination of parallel and serial work in multiple loops of the particle pushers, we used the OpenMP `loop` construct with appropriate thread-set binding. Considering the scenario that a loop should run sequentially using just one thread, we use `omp loop bind(thread)` to make sure a single thread runs this loop on GPU. Listing 1.1 is an example in which a nested loop runs sequentially while the outer loop is parallelized across teams and threads in the particle pushers. In line 1, the `target data` construct includes a `map` clause with the specifier `to` to copy data to the GPU target device and the specifier `tofrom` to copy data to the GPU and then back from the GPU at the end of the target data region. In line 2, `target teams loop` with `thread_limit` will parallelize the loop over teams and threads. The `thread_limit` clause was only used as a workaround for a NVIDIA compiler bug, explained later, because without that, each team would use only 1 thread. The variables `rhox` and `rhoy` are specified as `private` to provide an uninitialized variable to each thread. In line 5, `omp loop bind(thread)` causes the loop from line 6 to 8 to run sequentially by each thread in the team. Finally, the `omp atomic update` directive is used to enable multiple threads to safely update certain shared variables.

Listing 1.1. Example OpenMP GPU offloading code with a combination of parallel and serial work in the particle pushers.

```
1  !$omp target data map(to:psi(:)) map(tofrom:mypfl_es(:),
       mypfl_em(:) ,...)
2  !$omp target teams loop private(rhox,rhoy) thread_limit
       (128)
3  do m=1,mm_of_ns
4     ... // calculation of parameters
5  !$omp loop bind(thread)
6     do l=1,lr(1)
7        ... // calculation of parameters
8     enddo
9     ... // calculation of parameters
10    !$omp atomic update
11       mypfl_es(k)=...
12    !$omp end atomic
13    !omp atomic update
14       mypfl_em(k)=...
15    !$omp end atomic
16    ... // calculation of parameters
17 enddo
18 !$omp end target teams loop
19 !$omp end target data
```

Additionally, an example code related to the `reduction` clause in the shift is presented in Listing 1.2.

Listing 1.2. Example OpenMP GPU offloading code with `reduction` in the shift.

```
1  !$omp target data map(to:s_counts)
2     s_buf_length=0
3  !$omp target teams loop reduction(+:s_buf_length)
4     do i=0,nvp-1
```

```
5         s_buf_length=s_buf_length+s_counts(i)
6   enddo
7   !$omp end target teams loop
8   !$omp end target data
```

As mentioned previously, we have optimized the GEM code using OpenACC GPU offloading. We briefly discuss OpenMP and OpenACC similarities and our approach to ensure consistent OpenMP and OpenACC ports.

We have found that the NVIDIA compiler parallelizes code in the same way whether using omp target teams loop or acc loop gang vector. Similarly omp loop bind(thread) has the same functionality as acc loop seq, and omp atomic update corresponds to acc atomic update. Additionally, the reduction clause in OpenMP and OpenACC provides the same functionality. Note that in the initialization and shift of the GEM code, data movement directives are frequently used. Moreover, in order to ensure correct data movement by which the OpenMP results are consistent with OpenACC ones, the following two methods are utilized. The first is to compare the NVIDIA compiler -Minfo diagnostic reports for OpenMP and OpenACC, respectively, and find out whether there is any variable improperly specified or even not specified by data movement directives. The second is to compare the program output of each MPI rank at the end of each loop in OpenACC and OpenMP ports after calling MPI_Barrier. If there is a problem, modify the data movement or loop directives until the compiler diagnostics and runtime output are consistent between OpenMP and OpenACC.

3   The Structure of GEM

GEM uses a second-order Runge-Kutta method to advance the particle trajectories. In the prediction step, particles coordinates are evolved for a half time-step to $t^{n+1/2} = t^n + \triangle t/2$, using the field values at the end of the previous time step. The field equations are solved at $t^{n+1/2}$. In the correction step, particle coordinates are advanced from t^n to t^{n+1} using the field values at the half time-step. The corresponding FORTRAN subroutines are ppush and cpush. Each of these subroutines consists of a loop over all the particles that performs the time advance, followed by calls to subroutines (pp_init and pmove) that sort particles into the correct domains after their z-coordinates are updated (z is the direction along the magnetic field line, and is the dimension for the primary domain decomposition). A deposition is invoked after each pusher step to deposit particle charges onto the grids. The subroutine for this deposition is grid1, which consists of loops over particles and atomic data writing to the grids. Field solving is done after each deposition, and is done in the subroutine poisson. At present field solving is performed on CPU only.

4 Results and Analysis

4.1 Speedup Performance and Roofline Analysis for Single Node

In order to illustrate the speedup performance of OpenMP GPU offloading, we used a single node and compared against the baseline OpenMP CPU and OpenACC GPU implementations. The grid size is chosen to be $258 \times 16 \times 6$, where 6 corresponds to 6 GPUs per node on Summit, and the total particle number is 512 times the number of grid points. At present poisson kernel has not been ported to GPUs. We plan to use cuBLAS to offload this kernel to GPU in the future. Thus, poisson is excluded from Figs. 1 and 2. From Fig. 1, we found that the maximum speedup of $\sim 280.3X$ is achieved by ppush, which corresponds to the wallclock time decreasing from 17.9414 s for OpenMP CPU to 0.0640 s for OpenMP GPU offloading. Following ppush, cpush has a decrease of wallclock time from 18.4293 s to 0.0686 s, achieving a $\sim 268.6X$ speedup. Then, for grid1, the wallclock time decreases from 19.4655 s to 0.0787 s, corresponding to a $\sim 247.3X$ speedup. Note that ppush, cpush and grid1 have the same large loop structure parallelized by the loop construct and are using atomic operations. As it can be seen, the speedup for pmove is relatively small. The wallclock time for pmove decreases from 16.5079 s to 3.7956 s, a $\sim 4.3X$ speedup. Moreover, the speedup for total time is $\sim 19.6X$, with the wallclock time decreasing from 81.2744 s to 4.2084 s.

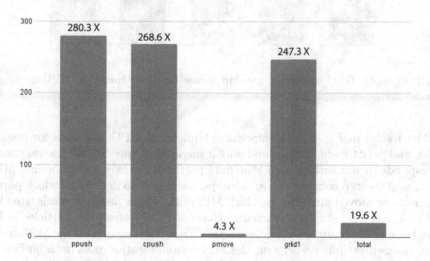

Fig. 1. OpenMP GPU offloading speedup versus baseline OpenMP CPU on single node.

Figure 2 shows the comparison between OpenMP GPU offloading and OpenACC GPU offloading. We note that OpenACC is slightly faster than OpenMP. ppush, cpush, and grid1 achieve almost the same acceleration performance for OpenMP and OpenACC while ~$0.7X$ speedup is obtained by pmove for OpenMP. Moreover, the total time for OpenACC GPU offloading is 3.2368 s, corresponding to ~$0.8X$ speedup for OpenMP. For pmove, in OpenMP GPU offloading, an additional data update between CPU and GPU can, so far, not be avoided, leading to an ~$0.7X$ slower runtime compared with OpenACC. This could be due to a compiler bug or due to some data management that is done automatically in OpenACC GPU offloading but needs to be explicitly prescribed in OpenMP GPU offloading, the oversight of which would make this an OpenMP programming bug we have to correct. This will be investigated in the future.

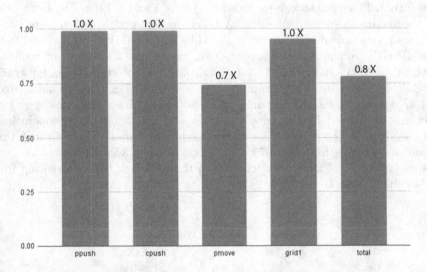

Fig. 2. OpenMP GPU offloading speedup versus baseline OpenACC GPU on single node.

The results in Fig. 1 show impressive triple-digit GPU speedups for ppush, cpush and grid1 code sections and only a single-digit speedup for pmove. pmove corresponds to the sorting step that puts particles in their corresponding MPI domains. This step consists of two substeps, the first is to determine which particles are to be moved and if so, to which MPI rank. This substep is accelerated by GPUs. The second step is to exchange the coordinates of all the particles to be moved and restructure the particle arrays. This is done among all the MPI ranks along the z-direction. At present, the MPI communication uses data buffers in CPU memory, which must be updated from the GPU data buffers. The message sizes are proportional to the total number of particles per MPI rank, and are constant in a weak scaling study. This leads to the poor performance of pmove in Fig. 1. It is challenging to accelerate the second substep on GPU and our algorithm needs to be rethought to avoid many small GPU kernel launches, excessive data movement between CPU and GPU, and to take advantage of GPUDirect communication capabilities. This will be the focus of future work. At the current time, it is instructive to look at a Roofline Model plot [8] to understand how the GPU has significantly accelerated certain GEM code sections.

Figure 3 shows a Roofline Model plot of the three kernels within `ppush`, `cpush` and `grid1` code sections. The plot shows that all 3 kernels have high enough arithmetic intensity to put them in the compute-bound region of the Roofline Model. The kernels are therefore limited by compute throughput, which is not typical of many scientific codes. The characteristics of our kernels are very high register usage per thread: `cpush` (244), `ppush` (244), and `grid1` (128). This limits the number of concurrent thread blocks per Streaming Multiprocessor (SM) to 2 for `cpush` and `ppush` kernels and 4 for `grid1` kernel on an NVIDIA V100 GPU. This is likely an impediment to our performance because our kernels contain hundreds of lines of code consisting of many high latency instructions and Fortran intrinsics, e.g. divide, exp, sqrt, modulus, min, max, sign and anint. It is possible we can improve performance by making the computations more concise in order to reduce the register count, enabling higher occupancy. If this is not possible we may be able to modify the computation to avoid the use of certain Fortran intrinsics that we find lead to most stalls on the GPU. The other impediment to performance is a large fraction of uncoalesced memory accesses. This is not a huge performance penalty for us because many memory requests are serviced by L2 cache rather than device memory. However, it indicates that there is room to further optimize performance on GPUs if we can improve the memory access pattern.

4.2 Scalability Analysis

In this section we show results from a weak scaling study with a fixed grid size and increased particle number. This shows the multi-node scalability of the GEM code. Herein, we used Summit and a grid size of $258 \times 64 \times 48$, where 48 is a multiple of 6. The particle number per grid cell is increased from 256 to 2048 in proportion to the node count being increased from 64 to 512. Figure 4 illustrates wallclock time for the different kernels with increasing number of nodes for GEM for OpenMP GPU offloading with NVIDIA HPC SDK 21.7. We found that the total time for different number of nodes is in the range of 2.0703 s for 64 nodes to 2.2583 s for 512 nodes. In general, `pmove` accounts for the largest proportion of the total time. `others`, which includes initiation of variables, is the second. Then, `grid1`, `ppush` and `cpush` occupy relatively small proportion.

In order to investigate the acceleration performance difference between GPU and CPU, Fig. 5 presents the results of OpenMP CPU. It is found that OpenMP GPU offloading is significantly faster than OpenMP CPU. The average OpenMP GPU offloading wallclock time for `ppush` is approximately 0.0221 s, which indicates $\sim 189.1X$ speedup compared with the CPU version. Additionally, `cpush` achieves $\sim 180.4X$ speedup while $\sim 208.9X$ speedup is obtained for `grid1`. Note that the extent of speedup closely corresponds to Fig. 1. The average OpenMP GPU offloading wallclock time for `pmove` is 1.6687 s, corresponding to $\sim 5.2X$ speedup compared with OpenMP CPU. In addition, the speedup for the average total time is $\sim 13.9X$ by comparing 2.1417 s for OpenMP GPU offloading with

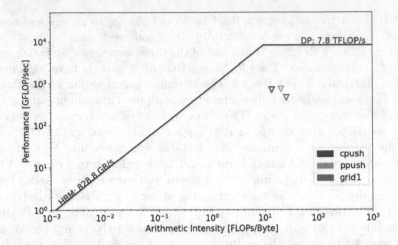

Fig. 3. A Roofline Model plot of three kernels on an NVIDIA V100 GPU. The plot shows that all kernels are in the compute-bound region and are limited by compute throughput. The kernels are given the same name as the GEM code section to improve readability. The plot was generated using a modified version of the script at [9] using data generated on Summit.

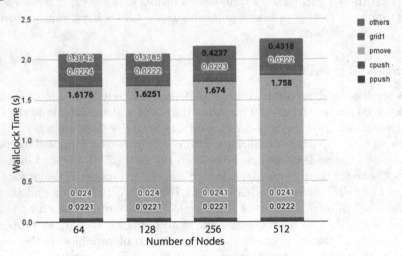

Fig. 4. Wallclock time for ppush, cpush, pmove, grid1, and others as a function of number of nodes for OpenMP GPU offloading with NVIDIA HPC SDK 21.7 on Summit.

29.8464 s for OpenMP CPU. Figure 6 illustrates the speedup of OpenMP GPU offloading as a function of number of nodes. It is found that with the increase of number of nodes, the speedup initially increases from ~13.7X for 64 nodes to the maximum of ~14.6X for 128 nodes, then decreases to ~14.0X for 256 nodes and ~13.4X for 512 nodes.

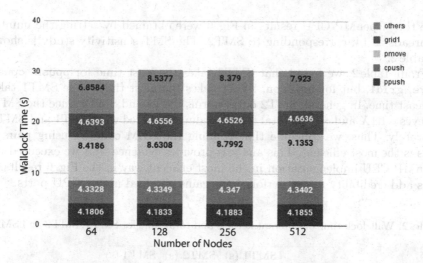

Fig. 5. Wallclock time for ppush, cpush, pmove, grid1, and others as a function of number of nodes for OpenMP CPU with NVIDIA HPC SDK 21.7 on Summit.

4.3 Investigation of Hardware Threads

Hardware Threads are supported by the IBM POWER9 processor on Summit and each of the POWER9's physical cores consists of 4 "slices". Knowing that 7 rows of cores are assigned for the compute node, in order to investigate different Simultaneous Multi Threading (SMT) modes, we set the number of threads in batch script as 7×4 for SMT4, 7×2 for SMT2 and 7×1 for SMT1, separately.

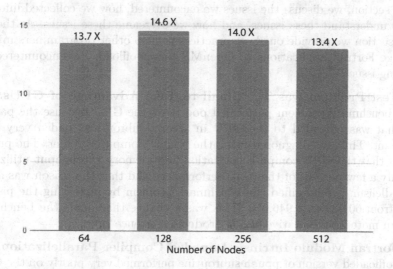

Fig. 6. OpenMP GPU offloading speedup versus baseline OpenMP CPU as a function of number of nodes with NVIDIA HPC SDK 21.7 on Summit.

Note that OpenMP CPU results in Fig. 6 were obtained by setting the number of threads as 14, corresponding to SMT2. The SMT sensitivity study is shown in Table 2.

From Table 2, we found that SMT2 takes the least time for ppush, cpush, pmove, grid1, but for poisson, SMT2 takes the most time while SMT1 takes the least time. In general, SMT2 outperforms SMT1 and SMT4 since the SMT2 achieves $\sim 1.1X$ and $\sim 1.2X$ total time speedup compared with SMT1 and SMT4, separately. Thus, we conclude that running the GEM code by using pairs of slices is the most efficient. This analysis provides evidence that we executed the OpenMP CPU implementation in the most efficient way in the Fig. 6 results. It helps add credibility to the performance gains obtained in our GPU ports.

Table 2. Wallclock time of different kernels and total time for SMT1, SMT2 and SMT4

	SMT1 (s)	SMT2 (s)	SMT4 (s)
ppush	4.5835	**4.1844**	4.9165
cpush	4.6725	**4.3387**	5.1464
pmove	10.3401	**8.746**	9.9178
grid1	4.9236	**4.6528**	6.018
poisson	**0.6487**	0.7149	0.6736
total	33.5194	**30.5613**	35.7715

5   Discussion

In this section, we discuss the issues we encountered, how we collected information to understand these issues, and how we overcame these issues. At the end of the section we provide our best practices to help other programmers migrating large Fortran applications to OpenMP target offload. We encountered the following issues:

The Test Problem was Too Small to Take Advantage of GPUs. Our initial benchmark problem performed poorly on the GPU because the particle loop that was offloaded to the GPU in several subroutines had a very short trip count. This was diagnosed using the Nsight Compute profiler. The profiler showed that the GPU compute utilization and memory throughput utilization was only a few percent of the peak performance and that the reason was a lack of parallelism. We modified the benchmark problem by increasing the particle count from 60,928 to 1,946,070. This was a change that made the benchmark problem more representative of our production science runs.

The Fortran Modulo Intrinsic Impeded Compiler Parallelization. Our initial offloaded version of ppush subroutine performed very poorly on the GPU. The Nsight Compute profiler showed that the kernel launch configuration used only 1 thread per thread block, i.e. 1 OpenMP thread per team. There should be no reason for a compiler or runtime to choose 1 OpenMP thread per thread block given that the loop trip count was 1,946,070. We found that we could increase the threads per team using the `thread_limit` clause. However, this is not a satisfactory way to write the code. We only found the underlying cause of the issue by closely looking at the output of the NVIDIA compiler `-Minfo` diagnostic. The diagnostic showed that the compiler was only parallelizing the loop over teams: ``Loop parallelized across teams ! blockidx%x''. We commented out code from the target region until the message changed to: ``Loop parallelized across teams, threads(128) ! blockidx%x threadidx%x''. We found that the Fortran `modulo` intrinsic was the culprit. This is a intrinsic that is not often used in Fortran codes and was never properly supported on the GPU by NVIDIA. This has been reported to NVIDIA. Our temporary workaround is to use the more often used `mod` intrinsic with slightly modified arguments in order to obtain correct results.

The Fortran Save Attribute Caused a Compiler Segfault. The initial version of our code used the `target teams distribute parallel do` combined directive. This caused the NVIDIA HPC SDK 21.7 compiler to segfault. We replaced the `target teams distribute parallel do` combined directive with the `target teams loop` combined directive and the compiler correctly compiled the code. We have reported this issue to NVIDIA. We have since found that the `save` attribute on module level variables caused the issue. This was hard to track down because GEM subroutines use many variables defined in modules. Once again our approach was to comment out code until the compiler segfault went away.

Improper Use of the map Clause Greatly Diminished Performance. The initial version of several of our offloaded code regions mapped a loop upper bound variable to the GPU. The Nsight Compute profiler showed that these kernels were launched on the GPU with 8 thread blocks despite the loop trip count being 1,946,070. We removed the `map` clause so that the variables were given an implicit data sharing attribute of `firstprivate` in the target region. This enabled the OpenMP runtime to use a more optimal launch configuration based on the value of the loop upper bound. When the variable was mapped, the OpenMP runtime correctly assumed that the host value could be different to the device value and fell back to using the default launch configuration for when loop bounds are unknown. We have since discussed this with NVIDIA. The NVIDIA compiler engineers said this was expected behavior but plan to tweak the default launch configuration from 8 thread blocks to 1024 thread blocks when loop bounds are unknown.

We have explained four issues that we encountered in the GEM code when using OpenMP target offload with the NVIDIA HPC SDK 21.7 compiler. These issues never appeared to us as standalone issues as our explanation above implies. This made it harder for us to understand the reasons for the poor kernel launch configurations until we understood each individual issue. Therefore, the best piece of advice to give programmers is to do experimentation with mini-apps rather than the full application. It would have made things easier if there was a mini-app that could run in a short amount of time, without MPI parallelization, without FFT library and ADIOS library dependencies, and just included the important subroutines without a large number of module-scoped variables that OpenMP compilers must appropriately handle in OpenMP target regions. This is important especially when using Fortran OpenMP target offload because Fortran support is less mature than C/C++ support in compilers. A mini-app would have enabled us to more quickly debug the issues and do more experimentation to understand performance.

•We recommend that programmers become familiar with the tools that different compilers provide. For example, the NVIDIA compiler provides the -Minfo diagnostic which gives information about how OpenMP loops are parallelized over thread blocks and threads on an NVIDIA GPU. Similarly, there is an environment variable named NVCOMPILER_ACC_NOTIFY=1 which gives terse information about kernel launch configurations. This was important for us because it saved us having to repeat the expensive Nsight Compute profiles while we were experimenting with different ideas to improve the kernel launch configuration. Finally, it is helpful if programmers have a basic understanding of GPU hardware and lower-level GPU programming approaches. Programmers need to be aware that GPUs are only useful when executing sufficient parallel work. Familiarity with CUDA is also helpful to understand the hierarchy of thread blocks and threads on an NVIDIA GPU. Our familiarity with CUDA enabled us to understand why mapping loop bounds greatly diminished performance. CUDA programmers know that kernels can access variables that were copied to global memory using cudaMemcpy and can also access variables that were passed by value as kernel arguments. These correspond to mapping a variable and making a variable firstprivate, respectively. An understanding of these lower-level concepts enabled us to successfully use a higher-level approach, in this case OpenMP, to achieve high performance on a GPU. We anticipate that other programmers can achieve success in the same way as us.

6   Summary

The principal contributions in this paper can be summarized as follows:

1. We have ported the GEM code, written in FORTRAN, by converting OpenACC GPU offloading to OpenMP GPU offloading. Additionally, we have kept all the particle and field data in GPU memory and minimized the data transfers between CPU and GPU.
2. We have compared OpenMP GPU with OpenMP CPU on Summit using a single node. Speedups as large as $\sim280.3X$ (i.e., ppush) can be achieved by using OpenMP GPU offloading compared with OpenMP CPU.
3. We have used weak scaling to compare OpenMP GPU with OpenMP CPU. The speedup for different kernels are very similar to that of a single node, and the speedup for total time could reach $\sim13.9X$.

4. We have investigated the hardware threads for IBM POWER9 processors on Summit, and indicated that SMT2 is the most efficient to run the OpenMP CPU cases.
5. We have discussed the issues we confronted when porting GEM on Summit using OpenMP GPU offloading, and explained explicitly the solutions.

In the future, the second substep of pmove would be optimized by avoiding excessive small GPU kernel launches, minimizing data movement between CPU and GPU, and utilizing GPUDirect communication capabilities. Additionally, cuBLAS would be coupled with poisson for calculating matrix operations on GPUs. Considering that DGX system consists of the latest generation of NVIDIA Tesla GPU A100, the comparison of the acceleration performance between A100 and V100 is of significant interest. Finally, we plan to explore whether converting GEM to C++ could improve performance and portability on future exascale platforms.

Acknowledgment. This research was supported by Exascale Computing Project (17-SC-20-SC), a collaborative effort of the U.S. Department of Energy Office of Science and the National Nuclear Security Administration, and Scientific Discovery through Advanced Computing (SciDAC) Center for Hogh Fidelity Boundary Plasma Simulation (HBPS) (DE-SC-000801).

This research used resources of the Oak Ridge Leadership Computing Facility at the Oak Ridge National Laboratory (ORNL) and resources of the National Energy Research Scientific Computing Center (NERSC), which are supported by the Office of Science of the U.S. Department of Energy under Contract Nos. DE-AC05-00OR22725 and DE-AC02-05CH11231, respectively.

References

1. Chen, Y., Parker, S.E.: A δf particle method for gyrokinetic simulations with kinetic electrons and electromagnetic perturbations. J. Comput. Phys. **189**(2), 463–475 (2003). https://doi.org/10.1016/S0021-9991(03)00228-6, https://www.sciencedirect.com/science/article/pii/S0021999103002286
2. Chen, Y., Parker, S.E.: Electromagnetic gyrokinetic δf particle-in-cell turbulence simulation with realistic equilibrium profiles and geometry. J. Comput. Phys. **220**(2), 839–855 (2007). https://doi.org/10.1016/j.jcp.2006.05.028
3. Cheng, J., et al.: Spatial core-edge coupling of the particle-in-cell gyrokinetic codes GEM and XGC. Phys. Plasmas **27**(12), 122510 (2020). https://doi.org/10.1063/5.0026043
4. Ku, S., et al.: A fast low-to-high confinement mode bifurcation dynamics in the boundary-plasma gyrokinetic code XGC1. Phys. Plasmas **25**(5), 056107 (2018)
5. Ku, S., Hager, R., Chang, C.S., Kwon, J., Parker, S.E.: A new hybrid-Lagrangian numerical scheme for gyrokinetic simulation of tokamak edge plasma. J. Comput. Phys. **315**, 467–475 (2016)
6. Manuilskiy, I., Lee, W.W.: The split-weight particle simulation scheme for plasmas. Phys. Plasmas **7**(5), 1381–1385 (2000). https://doi.org/10.1063/1.873955

7. Vergara Larrea, V.G., Budiardja, R.D., Gayatri, R., Daley, C., Hernandez, O., Joubert, W.: Experiences in porting mini-applications to OpenACC and OpenMP on heterogeneous systems. Concurr. Comput. Pract. Exp. **32**(20), e5780 (2020). https://doi.org/10.1002/cpe.5780, https://onlinelibrary.wiley.com/doi/abs/10.1002/cpe.5780
8. Williams, S., Waterman, A., Patterson, D.: Roofline: an insightful visual performance model for multicore architectures. Commun. ACM **52**(4), 65–76 (2009)
9. Yang, C.: Roofline methodology for NVIDIA GPUs, September 2020. https://gitlab.com/NERSC/roofline-on-nvidia-gpus

Author Index

Printed in the United States
by Baker & Taylor Publisher Services

Printed in the United States
by Baker & Taylor Publisher Services